United States
Department of
Agriculture

Forest Service

Pacific Southwest
Research Station

General Technical
Report
PSW-GTR-207

January 2008

Los Angeles 1-Million Tree Canopy Cover Assessment

E. Gregory McPherson, James R. Simpson, Qingfu Xiao, Chunxia Wu

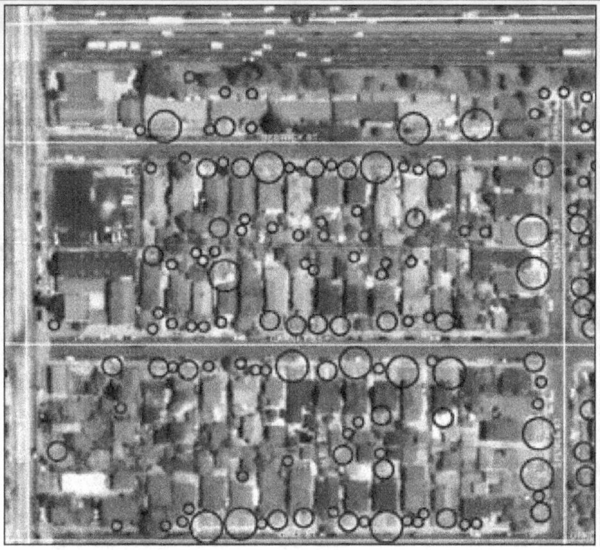

Authors

E. Gregory McPherson is a research forester and **James R. Simpson** is a forest meteorologist, U.S. Department of Agriculture, Forest Service, Pacific Southwest Research Station, Center for Urban Forest Research, Department of Plant Sciences, MS-6, University of California, Davis, One Shields Ave., Davis, CA 95616; **Qingfu Xiao** is a research hydrologist and **Chunxia Wu** is a post-doctoral researcher, Department of Land, Air, and Water Resources, University of California, Davis, One Shields Ave., Davis, CA 95616.

Abstract

McPherson, E. Gregory; Simpson, James R.; Xiao, Qingfu; Wu, Chunxia.
2008. Los Angeles 1-million tree canopy cover assessment. Gen. Tech. Rep.
PSW-GTR-207. Albany, CA: U.S. Department of Agriculture, Forest Service,
Pacific Southwest Research Station. 52 p.

The Million Trees LA initiative intends to chart a course for sustainable growth
through planting and stewardship of trees. The purpose of this study was to measure Los Angeles's existing tree canopy cover (TCC), determine if space exists for
1 million additional trees, and estimate future benefits from the planting. High-
resolution QuickBird remote sensing data, aerial photographs, and geographic
information systems were used to classify land cover types, measure TCC, and
identify potential tree planting sites. Benefits were forecast for planting of 1 million
trees between 2006 and 2010, and their growth and mortality were projected until
2040. Two scenarios reflected low (17 percent) and high (56 percent) mortality rates.
Numerical models were used with geographic data and tree size information for
coastal and inland climate zones to calculate annual benefits and their monetary
value. Los Angeles's existing TCC was 21 percent, and ranged from 7 to 37 percent
by council district. There is potential to add 2.5 million additional trees to the existing population of approximately 10.8 million, but only 1.3 million of the potential
tree sites are deemed realistic to plant. Thus, there is space for planting 1 million
new trees. Benefits for the 1-million-tree planting for the 35-year period were $1.33
billion and $1.95 billion for the high- and low-mortality scenarios, respectively.
Average annual benefits were $38 and $56 per tree planted. Eighty-one percent of
total benefits were aesthetic/other, 8 percent were stormwater runoff reduction, 6
percent energy savings, 4 percent air quality improvement, and less than 1 percent
atmospheric carbon reduction. Recommendations included developing a decision-
support tool for tree selection and tracking, as well as establishing a model parking
lot greening program.

Keywords: Ecosystem services, urban forestry, Los Angeles, tree canopy cover,
tree benefits.

Executive Summary

Mayor Antonio Villaraigosa of the city of Los Angeles, California, has charted a course for sustainable growth, and the region's community forest is a critical component of that vision. On September 30, 2006, the mayor kicked off his plan to plant 1 million trees over the next several years. The Million Trees LA initiative demonstrates the relevance of community forestry to the environmental, social, and economic health of Los Angeles.

To assist the city of Los Angeles, the USDA Forest Service Center for Urban Forest Research has conducted the study presented here to (1) measure existing tree canopy cover (TCC), (2) characterize potential TCC to determine the feasibility of planting 1 million trees, and (3) estimate future benefits from planting 1 million new trees. The study area is the city of Los Angeles (473 mi^2, population 3.7 million), excluding mountainous areas. Results are reported citywide and for the 15 council districts and 86 neighborhood councils.

High-resolution QuickBird remote sensing data, aerial photographs, geographic information systems (GIS), and image-processing software were used to classify land cover types, measure TCC, and identify potential tree planting sites. The accuracy assessment found that overall land cover classification accuracy was 88.6 percent based on a pixel-by-pixel comparison. The accuracy for classifying existing TCC was 74.3 percent.

One unique aspect of this study was "training" the computer to follow rules for locating potential planting sites, then drawing a circle for each small (15-ft crown diameter), medium (30 ft), and large (50 ft) tree site. Ground-truthing of 55 parcels led to calibration of the computer-generated estimates. Realistic TCC targets were determined for each council district with the goal of filling 50 percent of the available planting sites. This TCC target recognizes that each council district is unique because it has a different land use mix, as well as different existing and potential TCC that reflects historical patterns of development and tree stewardship. Each council district can do its "fair share" in helping the city meet its overall goal by filling 50 percent of its available tree planting sites. In so doing, council districts with the greatest number of empty planting sites will achieve the greatest relative increase in TCC, whereas those with higher stocking levels will obtain less enhancement.

Los Angeles's existing TCC is 21 percent, which compares favorably with 20 percent in Baltimore and 23 percent in New York City.

Los Angeles's existing TCC is 21 percent, which compares favorably with 20 percent in Baltimore and 23 percent in New York City. This finding is surprising given Los Angeles's Mediterranean climate, which makes irrigation essential for establishment and growth of many tree species. Other plantable space, such as irrigated grass and dry grass/bare soil, accounts for 12 and 6 percent of the city, respectively. Impervious (e.g., paving, roofs) and other surfaces (i.e., water) comprise the remaining 61 percent of the city's land cover (excluding mountainous areas). Hence, one-third of Los Angeles's land cover is either existing TCC or grass/bare soil with potential to become TCC. The number of existing trees is estimated to be 10.8 million assuming an average tree crown diameter of 16.4 ft.

At the council district level, TCC ranged from lows of 7 to 9 percent in council districts 9 and 15 to a high of 37 percent in council district 5. Tree canopy cover was strongly related to land use. As expected, low-density residential land uses had the highest TCC citywide (31 percent), whereas industrial and commercial land uses had the lowest TCC (3 to 6 percent).

Existing TCC exceeded 40 percent in three neighborhood councils: Bel Air-Beverly Crest (53 percent), Arroyo Seco (46 percent), and Studio City (42 percent). Neighborhood councils with the lowest TCC were Downtown Los Angeles (3 percent), Wilmington (5 percent), and Historic Cultural and Macarthur (6 percent).

There is potential to add 2.5 million additional trees or 12.4 percent TCC. Thus, "technical" potential for Los Angeles is 33.2 percent TCC, or about 13.3 million trees. However, it is not realistic to think that every possible tree site will be planted. Assuming a realistic target of filling about 50 percent of the unplanted sites results in adding 1.3 million more trees equivalent to a 6.7-percent increase in TCC. Hence, "market" potential is 27.5 percent TCC, or 12.1 million trees. Planting 1 million trees is feasible and if accomplished as indicated above, would saturate 97 percent of the existing market potential.

Benefits are forecast for a scenario that gradually increases the rate of the planting of 1 million trees between 2006 and 2010 and tracks their growth and mortality until 2040. Tree growth over the 35-year period is based on intensive measurements of predominant street tree species in Santa Monica for coastal Los Angeles, and in Claremont, for inland Los Angeles. Representative small, medium, and large species were selected for each zone to model growth, with nearly one-half of the trees small, 42 percent medium, and 9 percent large at maturity. Low- and high-mortality scenarios reflect effects of loss rates on tree numbers and associated benefits. After 35 years, the number of surviving trees is 828,924 and 444,889 for the two scenarios, respectively. In both scenarios, planted trees are distributed among land uses such that 55 percent are in low-density residential, 17 percent in institutional, 14 percent in medium/high-density residential, 9 percent in commercial, and 5 percent in industrial use.

Numerical models were used with geographic data and tree size information for the coastal and inland climate zones to calculate annual benefits and their monetary value. Benefits calculated on an annual basis and summed for the 35-year

Benefits calculated on an annual basis and summed for the 35-year period are $1.33 billion and $1.95 billion for the high- and low-mortality scenarios, respectively.

period are $1.33 billion and $1.95 billion for the high- and low-mortality scenarios, respectively. These values translate into $1,328 and $1,951 per tree planted, or $38 and $56 per tree per year when divided by the 35-year period. For the low-mortality scenario, 81 percent of total benefits are aesthetic/other, 8 percent are stormwater runoff reduction, 6 percent energy savings, 4 percent air quality improvement, and less than 1 percent atmospheric carbon reduction.

The distribution of benefits among council districts is closely related to the climate zone and the number of trees planted. Benefits per tree are about 50 percent less ($700 to $1,000 instead of $1,300 to $2,400) in the coastal zone (council districts 11 and 15) than the inland zone because the growth curve data indicate that the trees are smaller, air pollutant concentrations are lower, and building heating and cooling loads are less owing to the milder climate.

Aesthetic and other benefits. Citywide, aesthetic and other benefits ranged from $1.1 to $1.6 billion, or $1,100 to $1,600 per tree over the 35-year period for the high- and low-mortality scenarios. This amount reflects the economic contribution of trees to property sales prices and retail sales, as well as other benefits such as beautification, privacy, wildlife habitat, sense of place, and psychological and spiritual well-being.

Stormwater runoff reduction. By intercepting rainfall in their crowns, trees reduce stormwater runoff and protect water quality. The average annual interception rate per tree ranges from a low of 102 gal to a high of 1,481 gal based on tree size, rainfall amounts, and foliation period. Over the 35-year span of the project, 1 million trees will reduce runoff by approximately 13.5 to 21.3 billion gallons (1,810 to 2,840 million cubic ft). The value of this benefit ranges from $97.4 to $153.1 million for the high- and low-mortality scenarios, respectively.

Energy use reduction. By shading residential buildings and lowering summertime air temperatures, the 1 million trees are projected to reduce electricity consumed for air conditioning by 718,671 to 1.1 million MWh or $76 to $119 million for the high- and low-mortality scenarios. However, this cooling savings is partially offset by increased heating costs from tree shade that obstructs winter sunlight. Tree shade is expected to increase natural gas required for heating by 101,000 to 154,000 MBtu, which is valued at $674,000 to $1 million. Despite this cost, a net energy savings of $75.7 to $117.4 million is projected for the high- and low-mortality scenarios.

Atmospheric carbon dioxide reduction. Over the 35-year planning horizon, the 1 million trees are projected to reduce atmospheric carbon dioxide (CO_2) by 764,000 to 1.27 million tons, for the high- and low-mortality scenarios. Assuming this benefit is priced at $6.68 per ton, the corresponding value is $5.1 to $8.5

By improving air quality, the tree planting will enhance human health and environmental quality in Los Angeles. This benefit is valued at $53 to $83 million over the 35-year planning horizon. Interception of small particulate matter (PM_{10}) and uptake of ozone (O_3) and nitrogen dioxide (NO_2) are especially valuable.

million. Emission reductions at power plants associated with effects of the trees on building energy use (498,000 to 772,000 tons) are greater than biological sequestration of CO_2 by the trees themselves (389,000 to 598,000 tons). A relatively small amount of CO_2 is released during tree care and decomposition of dead biomass (101,000 to 123,000 tons). The CO_2 reduction benefit varies widely based on tree size. For example, in the inland zone for the low-mortality scenario, the small tree annually sequesters and reduces emissions by only 5 and 55 lb per tree on average, compared to 220 and 150 lb for the large tree.

Air quality improvement. By improving air quality, the tree planting will enhance human health and environmental quality in Los Angeles. This benefit is valued at $53 to $83 million over the 35-year planning horizon. Interception of small particulate matter (PM_{10}) and uptake of ozone (O_3) and nitrogen dioxide (NO_2) are especially valuable. The 1-million-tree planting project is estimated to intercept and reduce power plant emissions of particulate matter by 1,846 to 2,886 tons over the 35-year period for the high- and low-mortality scenarios, respectively. The value of this benefit ranges from $19 to $29 million, or 35 percent of total air quality benefits.

The 1 million trees are projected to reduce O_3 by 2,430 to 3,813 tons, with average annual deposition rates ranging from 0.25 to 0.35 lb per medium tree in the low-mortality scenario for the coastal and inland zones, respectively. Ozone uptake is valued at $17.9 to $28.1 million over the project life for the high- and low-mortality scenarios, or 34 percent of total air quality benefits.

Uptake of NO_2, an O_3 precursor, is estimated to range from 1,949 to 3,039 tons, with a value of $14.6 to $22.8 million for the high- and low-mortality scenarios over the 35-year period. This benefit accounts for 27 percent of the total air quality benefit. The small remaining benefit is reduced power plant emissions of volatile organic compounds from cooling energy savings.

We found that the benefit values reported here are reasonable when compared with previously reported findings from similar analyses for the same region. However, it is important to note limitations of this study and to identify sources of error. These limitations are discussed fully in the "Discussion" section of this report.

We conclude this study with a discussion of ways to successfully disseminate data, to implement the 1-million-trees program, and future research needs.

The Center for Urban Forest Research proposes a collaboration with other scientists in southern California to study the effects of trees on the social, economic, and environmental health of Los Angeles and its nearly 4 million residents. In particular, we need to better understand:

- Barriers to tree planting and incentives for different markets

As the second largest city in the United States, Los Angeles manages an extensive municipal forest. Its management should set the standard for the region and the country.

Los Angeles is a vibrant city that will continue to grow. As it grows, it should also continue to invest in its tree canopy.

- Effects of trees on the urban heat island and air quality
- Effects of drought stress on tree survival and ability to remove air pollutants
- Primary causes of tree mortality
- Best management practices to promote tree survival
- Citywide policy scenarios to promote urban tree canopy, neighborhood desirability, and economic development
- How to link TCC goals to other city goals: increasing community health, neighborhood quality of life, environmental literacy, and sustainability

As the second largest city in the United States, Los Angeles manages an extensive municipal forest. Its management should set the standard for the region and the country. Working cooperatively, the Center for Urban Forest Research and the city of Los Angeles could conduct a tree inventory and assessment that will establish a sound basis for future management aimed at increasing resource sustainability.

Los Angeles is a vibrant city that will continue to grow. As it grows, it should also continue to invest in its tree canopy. This is no easy task, given financial constraints and trends toward higher density development that may put space for trees at a premium. The challenge ahead is to better integrate the green infrastructure with the gray infrastructure by increasing tree planting, providing adequate space for trees, and designing plantings to maximize net benefits over the long term, thereby perpetuating a resource that is both functional and sustainable. The Center for Urban Forest Research looks forward to working with the city of Los Angeles and its many professionals to meet that challenge in the years ahead.

Contents

1   **Introduction**

1   Million Trees LA Initiative

2   Tree Canopy Cover Assessments

5   **Objectives**

5   **Methodology**

5   Study Site

6   Data Sets

7   Measuring Existing Tree Canopy Cover

9   Characterizing Potential and Target Tree Canopy Cover

11   Parking Lot Sampling

14   Tree Canopy Cover Target

15   The 1-Million-Tree Planting Scenario

15   Tree Data

16   Benefits

20   **Results**

20   Existing Tree Canopy Cover

24   Potential Tree Planting Sites and Target Tree Canopy Cover

28   Benefits From 1 Million Trees

32   Citywide Benefits by Benefits Type

37   **Discussion**

37   Comparison of Results

39   Uncertainty and Limitations

43   **Common and Scientific Names**

44   **Acknowledgments**

44   **Metric Equivalents**

45   **References**

50   **Appendix**

Introduction

Urbanization creates significant changes in land use and land cover, affecting the structure, pattern, and function of ecosystems. The public is increasingly concerned about how these changes influence daily life and affect the sustainability of "quality of life" for future generations. Improving air quality, alleviating water shortages, cooling urban heat islands, and reducing stormwater runoff are challenges facing Los Angeles. For example, between 627,800 and 1.48 million gastrointestinal illnesses are caused annually by swimming in contaminated beaches in southern California (Given et al. 2006). This public health impact corresponds to an economic loss of $21 to $51 million related to health care costs. Also, long-term effects of exposure to high air pollution levels in southern California have been associated with decreased respiratory health (Gauderman et al. 2004). Exposure to freeway-related pollutants has been found to impair children's lungs and is associated with increased asthma (Gauderman et al. 2005). Rapid growth in Los Angeles, with a population of nearly 4 million, is accelerating these problems. The problems need solutions as the region tries to protect and restore environmental quality while enhancing economic opportunity.

> **Long-term effects of exposure to high air pollution levels in southern California have been associated with decreased respiratory health.**

Tree canopy is a valuable component of Los Angeles's urban ecosystem (McBride and Jacobs 1986). Trees in urban settings are important to improving urban life, as well as human physical and emotional well-being. Research suggests that human beings have an innate affiliation to natural settings, a concept described as biophilia (Kellert and Wilson 1993). Numerous studies link access to living trees, outdoor air, and natural light to increased employee and student productivity, faster hospital recoveries, less crime, and an overall reduction in stress and anxiety. Thus, expanding the urban forest is part of the solution to Los Angeles's social, environmental, and economic problems—it is integral to enhancing public health programs, increasing land values and local tax bases, providing job training and employment opportunities, reducing costs of city services, increasing public safety, improving air quality, offsetting carbon emissions, managing stormwater runoff, mitigating water shortages, and conserving energy.

> **Expanding the urban forest is part of the solution to Los Angeles's social, environmental, and economic problems.**

Million Trees LA Initiative

Mayor Antonio Villaraigosa of the city of Los Angeles, California, has charted a course for sustainable growth, and the region's community forest is a critical component of that vision. On September 30, 2006, the mayor kicked off his plan to plant 1 million trees in the next several years. The Million Trees LA initiative demonstrates the relevance of community forestry to the environmental, social, and economic health of Los Angeles.

Tree Canopy Cover Assessments

Tree canopy cover (TCC) is the percentage of a site covered by the canopies of trees. Many communities are adopting TCC goals to maintain and improve forest cover. Advances in remote sensing technology and geographic information systems (GIS) make it practical to measure TCC on a periodic basis (Price et al. 2002, Xiao and McPherson 2005, Xiao et al. 2004). Vegetation has unique spectral reflectance characteristics with strong absorption in red wavelengths and strong reflectance in near-infrared wavelengths that allow distinction of trees from other ground surface covers.

Tree canopy cover has become a popular metric for several reasons. It is relatively easy to measure with remote sensing technology and less costly than field sampling. It is comparable across a city and among cities. The size of the area measured does not matter. The TCC is a good performance measure because it can be applied to detect change across space and time. Finally, TCC is an easy-to-understand concept that is useful in communicating to the public (Poracsky and Lackner 2004).

It is important to recognize the limitations associated with using TCC as a metric. The TCC is two dimensional, only indicating the spread of canopy across land surfaces. It does not provide information on the vertical extent of tree canopy, species composition, age diversity, or health. To describe the structure, function, and value of urban forests fully, data obtained from field sampling are required as well. For example, many functional benefits have been linked to the leaf surface area of trees, which is difficult to estimate with accuracy using only TCC. Moreover, predicting future trends in urban forest structure, function, and management needs requires a richer data set than TCC alone provides.

Accurately classifying TCC is difficult owing to the complex spatial assemblages of disparate patches of land cover types in urban settings. Urban areas are a mosaic of many different land covers, land uses, and built structures, each of which has different spectral reflectance characteristics (Gong and Howarth 1990). Unlike trees in rural forests that tend to form continuous canopies, trees in urban settings are often isolated or in small groups. The influence of background, such as soil and shadow, makes the problem of characterizing trees by remote sensing even more difficult. In such cases, high-resolution remotely sensed data are important for accurate TCC mapping (Xiao et al. 2004).

Many studies have used remote sensing data and GIS to map TCC. American Forests has used satellite imagery and CITYgreen GIS software to map historical TCC change, as well as the value of annual benefits from urban forests for cities such as Atlanta, Georgia, Washington, D.C., and Roanoke, North Carolina

(American Forests 2002a, 2002b, 2002c). Irani and Galvin (2003) used IKONOS data (13-ft spatial resolution) to map TCC in Baltimore, Maryland. Goetz and others (2003) found the accuracy of tree cover estimates mapped with IKONOS imagery in the mid-Atlantic region to be comparable to manual aerial photointerpretation. Poracsky and Lackner (2004) compared Portland's tree canopy in 1972, 1991, and 2002 by using TM and multispectral scanner data (100-ft plus resolution). High-resolution infrared photography and light detection and ranging (LIDAR) data were used to map TCC in Vancouver, Washington (Kaler and Ray 2005). Urban cover was mapped with 82 percent accuracy for Syracuse, New York, using high-resolution digital color-infrared imagery (Myeong et al. 2001), and similar data were used to assess New York City's TCC (Grove et al. 2006). Xiao et al. (2004) used AVIRIS (airborne visible infrared imaging spectrometer) data to map urban tree species in Modesto, California, but developing spectral signatures for each species was time consuming.

Potential TCC (PTCC) is the percentage of area on the ground without TCC that could be covered by additional tree canopy. Traditionally, PTCC is the amount of residual pervious surface, including all grass and bare soil. It does not include tree cover that could be achieved by adding trees to impervious surfaces like paved parking lots and plazas.

We differentiate between two other terms related to TCC, technical potential and market potential (McPherson 1993). Technical potential is the total amount of planting space—existing TCC plus pervious surfaces that could have trees (TCC + PTCC)—whereas market potential is the amount of TCC plus the amount of PTCC that is plantable given physical or preferential barriers that preclude planting. Physical barriers include conflicts between trees and other higher priority existing or future uses, such as sports fields, vegetable gardens, and development. Another type of market barrier is personal preference to keep certain locations free of TCC. Whereas technical potential is easily measured, market potential is a complex sociocultural phenomenon that has not been well studied. The only study we are aware of is a survey of nonparticipants of the Sacramento Shade program (Sar-kovich 2006). The two most common reasons customers chose not to accept a free shade tree were lack of space (34 percent), a physical constraint, and "Do Not Want Any More Trees" (25 percent), a personal preference. This finding applies primarily to low-density residential land uses and suggests that a substantial amount of PTCC is likely to remain tree-free because of market forces.

Communities set TCC targets as measurable goals that inform policies, ordinances, and specifications for land development, tree planting, and preservation. Targets should respond to the regional climate and local land use patterns. Climate is important because cities in regions where the amount of rainfall favors tree growth tend to have the most TCC. For example, mean TCC was higher in cities in naturally forested areas (31 percent) than in grasslands (19 percent) and deserts (10 percent) (Nowak et al. 1996). Within a city, land use is the dominant factor influencing TCC because it affects the amount of space available for vegetation. Residential land uses tend to have the greatest TCC, and commercial/industrial land uses have the least (Sanders 1984).

American Forests has developed the most widely adopted TCC targets. Their TCC targets reflect constraints posed by regional climate and land use patterns. Based on studies throughout the United States, American Forests developed generic TCC targets for temperate and arid climate cities (Kollin 2006). For arid cities such as Los Angeles, they recommend an average citywide TCC of 25 percent, with values of 35 percent for suburban zones, 18 percent for urban residential zones, and 9 percent for commercial land uses. Suggested TCC targets are substantially higher for temperate cities. Communities such as Roanoke, Virginia (Urban Forestry Task Force 2003), and Montgomery County, Maryland (Montgomery County 2000), have adopted American Forests' TCC targets.

In New York City, where existing TCC was 23 percent and another 43 percent of PTCC was identified, the TCC target was set at 30 percent (Grove et al. 2006) (fig. 1). The 30-percent target corresponded to an air quality modeling scenario employed in a related study (Luley and Bond 2002). Above this TCC target, there were no additional air pollutant reductions. In Baltimore, existing TCC was 20 percent and there was potential for another 53 percent TCC (Galvin et al. 2006). A 46-percent target TCC was recommended, filling about one-half of the remaining PTCC (fig. 1). This target was related to results from a remote sensing study that detected increased levels of stream health associated with greater watershed tree cover, although impervious cover was the primary predictive variable (Geotz et al. 2003). City leaders adopted a 40 percent TCC target, thinking that doubling the overall TCC from 20 to 40 percent was an easily understood goal. Different TCC targets were set for each land use in both New York City and Baltimore.

The cities of Portland, Oregon (Poracsky and Lackner 2004), and Vancouver, Washington (Kaler and Ray 2005), set TCC targets by land use corresponding to the 75th percentile of TCC, a value that falls mid-way in the range of the upper-half of TCC for polygons in each land use class (fig. 1). They found that TCC values were not normally distributed within land uses and, therefore, the mean value is not very representative. They selected the 75th percentile value as a target because it is both attainable—that value had been achieved or surpassed in 25 percent of the data set—and high enough to result in a noticeable expansion of TCC. Citywide TCC targets were set at 46 percent in Portland and 28 percent in Vancouver.

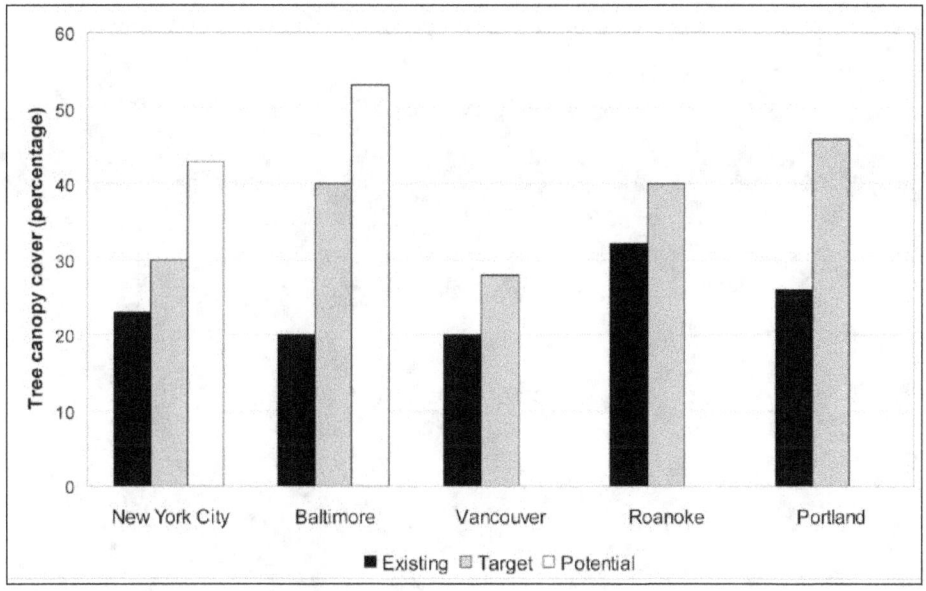

Figure 1—Existing, target, and potential tree canopy cover for five U.S. cities.

Objectives

The objectives of this study were to (1) measure existing TCC, (2) characterize PTCC to determine the feasibility of planting 1 million trees, and (3) estimate future benefits from planting 1 million new trees.

Methodology

Study Site

The city of Los Angeles was founded by the Spanish in 1781 and served as a colonial capital before incorporation in 1850. City development began in the late 1800s after arrival of the railroads and the discovery of oil in the 1890s. Today, Los Angeles is one of the largest metropolitan areas in the United States and is a major shipping, manufacturing, communications, financial, and distribution center noted for its entertainment industry (fig. 2). Like many coastal California cities, it is undergoing a period of rapid population growth and expansion.

Los Angeles (latitude: 34°06′ 36″ N, longitude: 118°24′ 40″ W) has a land area of 473 mi^2 and a population of 3,694,820 (U.S. Census Bureau 2000). There are 15 council districts and 86 neighborhood councils. Topographic gradients are small in the coastal areas and inland valleys; however, within the city limits there are mountain ranges with steep slopes. Elevation changes from sea level to 5,063 ft at Mount Lukens in the northeast corner of the city.

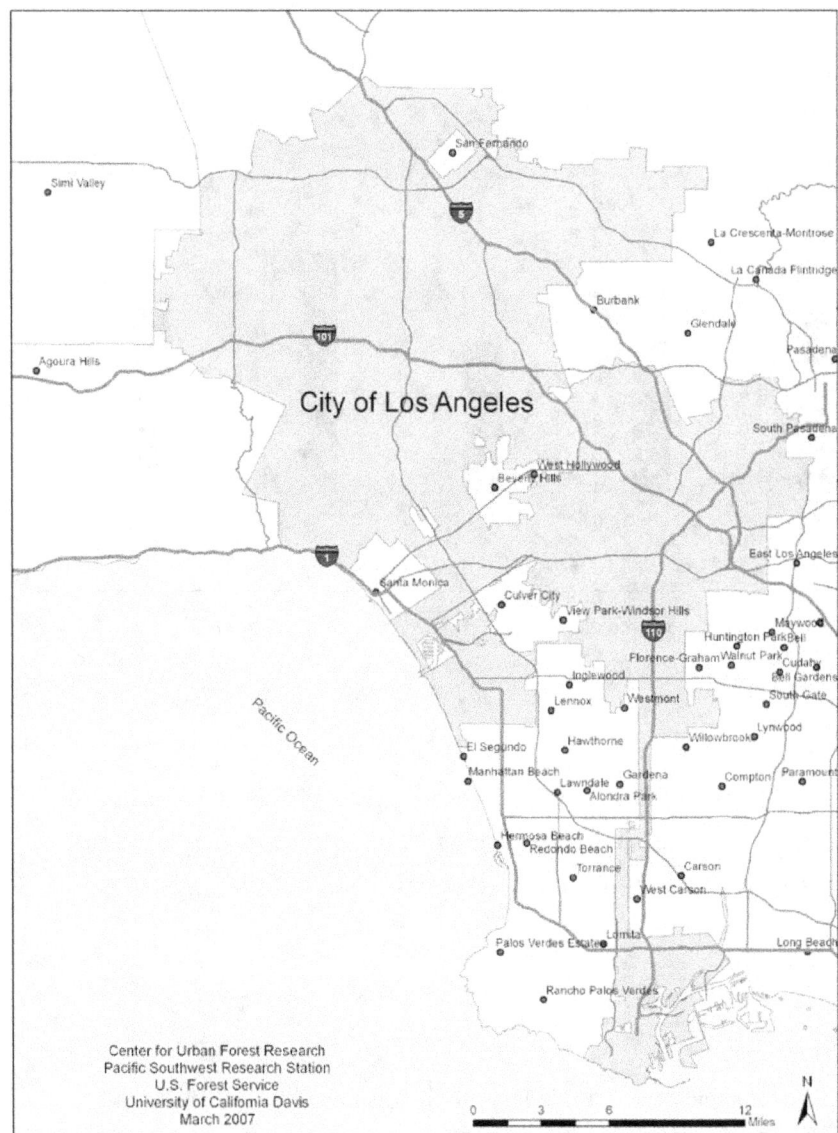

Figure 2—The city of Los Angeles.

Data Sets

Remote sensing data—

Very high spatial resolution remote sensing data were required to accurately map vegetation coverage and available tree planting sites at the parcel scale. QuickBird[1] satellite imagery (DigitalGlobe, Longmont, Colorado) was used with pixel resolutions of 2.0 ft for panchromatic data and 7.9 ft for multispectral data.

In this study, we demonstrate an important application of urban TCC mapping by combining remote sensing and GIS techniques.

---

[1] The use of trade names or firm names in this publication is for reader information and does not imply endorsement by the U.S. Department of Agriculture of any product or service.

In this study, we demonstrate an important application of urban TCC mapping by combining remote sensing and GIS techniques. Coupling GIS to the analysis of remote sensing data improves the accuracy of the results. Incorporating spatial location is a standard method for registering images to base maps (Ambrosia et al. 1998, Lakshmi et al. 1998, Shao et al. 1998).

Three types of remotely sensed data and several GIS data layers were used in this study. The QuickBird data included 82 scenes that were collected from 2002 to 2005. Most of these data were collected when deciduous trees were in leaf, but several images were collected during the transition periods of late March and early November. Aerial imagery included year 2000 black-and-white images at 6-in resolution (city of Los Angeles, California) and 2005 natural color images at 3-ft resolution (USDA Forest Service), both taken when trees were in leaf. The image-processing system ENVI (Environment for Visualizing Images, Research Systems, Lafayette, Colorado) was used for image analysis.

GIS data—

The GIS data layers were provided by the Public Works, Bureau of Engineering of the city of Los Angeles. Data layers included the boundaries of the city, neighborhood councils, council districts, parcels, parks, streets, and land uses. ArcGIS (Environmental Systems Research Institute) was used for mapping and other spatial analysis. All vegetation and potential tree planting sites were in ArcGIS format. Nine original land use classes were aggregated into six classes (table 1).

Measuring Existing Tree Canopy Cover

Initial data processing involved reassembling remote sensing and GIS data layers. The key elements of this step included georegistering remote sensing data and projecting all data to the California State Plane. The multispectral QuickBird data

> **Three types of remotely sensed data and several GIS data layers were used.**

Table 1—Nine land use classes aggregated into six

Final land use class	Original land use class
Unknown	Unknown
Low-density residential	Low-density housing
Medium/high-density residential	Medium-density housing
	High-density housing
Industrial	Heavy industry
	Light industry
Commercial	Neighborhood commerce
	Regional commerce
Institutional	Open space/public and quasi-public lands

were pan-sharpened (resampled by using a principal-components bilinear interpolation of a coarser resolution image) to produce a more defined image at 60-cm spatial resolution.

General classification processes—

Classification is a statistical process that groups homogeneous pixels into areas of interest based on common spectral characteristics. Two commonly used classification techniques are supervised (human-assisted) and unsupervised (clustering). Each method serves a particular purpose, and both methods were used in this study. We selected four land cover mapping types based on the objectives of this project: tree (tree and shrub), grass (green grass and ground cover), dry grass/bare soil (dry grass and bare soil), and impervious surface (includes pervious pavement).

Supervised classification used spectral angle mapper because it is a physically based spectral classification. Pixels were classified by using radiance rather than reflectance. Unsupervised classification automatically clusters pixels into classes with similar spectral signatures based on statistics, without any user-defined training classes. We used K-means, which calculates class means evenly distributed in the data space, then iteratively clusters the pixels into the nearest class by using a minimum-distance technique (Tou and Gonzalez 1974).

Data set masking—

Masking techniques have been widely used in urban vegetation mapping (Xiao et al. 2004) to reduce the possibility of confusion among cover classes. Three masks were used in this study. The first mask separated green vegetation. The second mask separated nonvegetation (i.e., pavements, buildings, water, and bare soil) and dry vegetation (i.e., unirrigated grass). The third mask separated areas with dry vegetation, bare soil, and other pavements where spectral mixing occurs. These masks were created based on NDVI (normalized difference vegetation index), the ratio of the reflectance difference between near-infrared (NIR) and red and the sum of the reflectance at NIR and red. The NDVI's threshold values for these masks varied from image to image because the QuickBird images were from several years.

The naturally vegetated mountains (50,208 acres) were digitized and masked out from the study area. We masked mountains because their land cover, vegetation management, and topographic gradient are different from those of the urban areas. A small part of the study area was covered with cloud cover and masked out (8,202 acres). Color aerial images replaced the QuickBird data in these areas.

Vegetation cover mapping—

Vegetation cover mapping included mapping tree cover, green grass cover, and dry grass cover. In this study, shrubs were treated as trees. The NDVI was used to distinguish vegetation and nonvegetation cover. We used unsupervised classification to separate mixed pixels containing vegetation and nonvegetation land cover types. In urban settings, most trees are planted in irrigated turf grass, where trees and the background cover have similar NDVI values. We used supervised classification to separate trees from irrigated grass.

Vegetation mapping accuracy assessment—
The accuracy of the classification models was assessed on a land cover type basis at pixel and parcel scales for a stratified random sample of 56 parcels based on land use (Nowak et al. 2003). Land cover types were digitized in each sample parcel from the Quickbird images as references for accuracy assessment. The pixel-scale analysis compared classified land cover types with digitized types by pixel. Over 1.5 million pixels were compared. The purpose of the parcel-scale analysis was to identify and eliminate problems caused by co-registration of different data layers. We compared the amount of each land cover area by parcel. The confusion matrix (Kohavi and Provost 1998, Xiao and McPherson 2005) was used to assess mapping accuracy.

Existing TCC and tree number estimates—
Existing TCC is presented at the citywide, council district, and neighborhood council levels. The number of existing trees is estimated assuming an average tree crown diameter of 16.4 ft, based on results from an intensive field study of trees throughout Sacramento, California (McPherson 1998).

Characterizing Potential and Target Tree Canopy Cover

Previous studies characterized PTCC as the amount of existing pervious surface (i.e., grass and bare soil) that is not tree cover. Instead of characterizing PTCC as the residual pervious area, we identify potential tree planting sites for individual trees of small (15-ft crown diameter), medium (30-ft crown diameter), and large (50-ft crown diameter) mature sizes. Data on the numbers and ratios of small, medium, and large trees are used to project future benefits from the 1-million-tree planting for trees with these mature sizes.

Decision rules for locating potential tree planting sites—
Although circle-packing algorithms have been developed to place circles into an empty space, they are hard to implement in ArcGIS given the many irregularly shaped polygons that could contain tree sites. We therefore developed a computer program to iteratively search, test, and locate potential tree planting sites. The program begins by masking out a 2-ft buffer around impervious surfaces to avoid conflicts with tree trunks and roots that are too close to buildings and paving. In

Previous studies characterized PTCC as the amount of existing pervious surface that is not tree cover. Instead of characterizing PTCC as the residual pervious area, we identify potential tree planting sites for individual trees of small, medium, and large mature sizes.

addition, restricted soil volumes in urban areas can limit tree survival and growth. The computer program therefore tests each potential planting site to ensure that each tree is allotted sufficient space to grow: 16 ft^2 of pervious surface for small trees, 36 ft^2 for medium trees, and 100 ft^2 for large trees. Because large trees produce proportionately greater benefits than small trees, the program starts by filling sites with large trees (50-ft crown diameters), then medium (30-ft crown diameter), and small (15-ft) trees. The program "draws" a 25-ft no-planting buffer around existing TCC to avoid overlapping crowns from potential trees with 50-ft crown diameters. It then "draws" the circular crowns of appropriately scaled 50-ft trees beginning in the center of each polygon. This procedure is repeated several times for 50-ft trees, with buffers redrawn each time to eliminate overlap with crowns of previously located planting sites for new 50-ft trees. The process is then repeated for 30-ft and 15-ft trees (fig. 3).

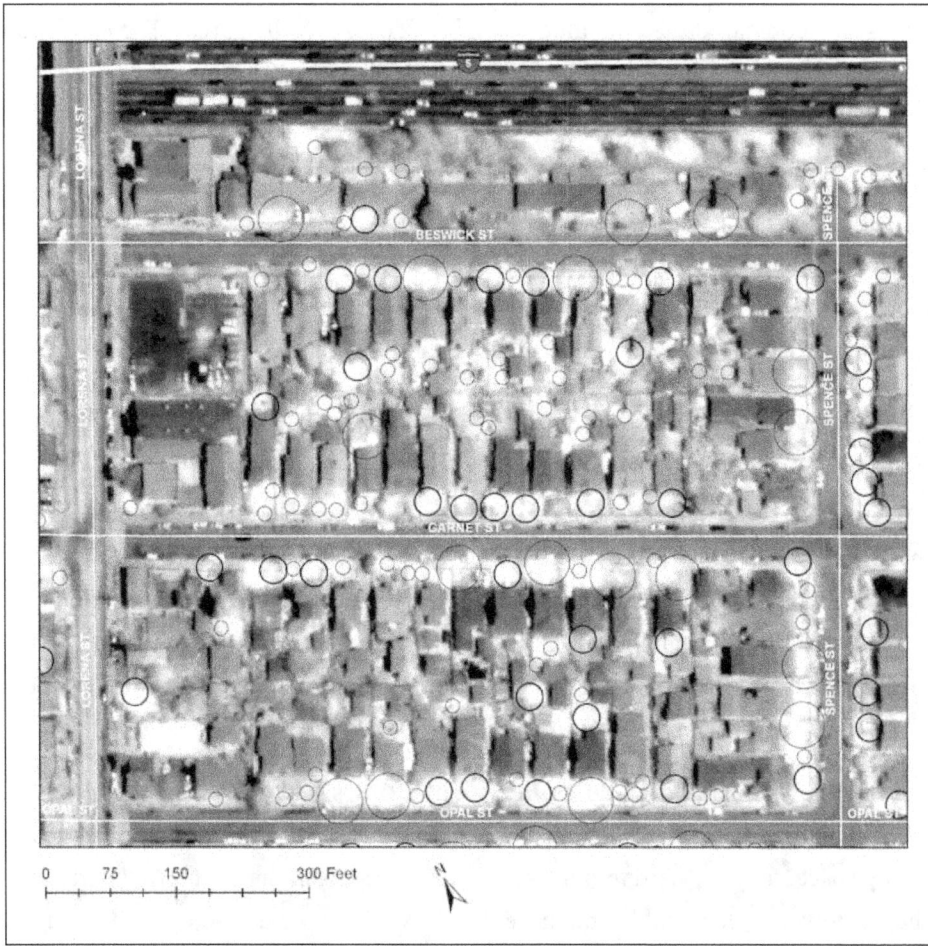

Figure 3—Potential tree planting sites in a Los Angeles neighborhood as identified by the tree-planting algorithm.

Parking Lot Sampling

Parking lots cover a large area of Los Angeles and represent an important tree planting opportunity. However, distinguishing parking lots from other impervious surfaces (e.g., buildings and roads) is difficult because they are constructed from similar materials. Using remotely sensed data to identify parking lots and potential tree planting sites was not feasible given the resources at hand. Therefore, we decided to identify the amount of paved area that could be available for tree planting based on a sample of parking lots located throughout the city. We focused on large parking lots ($>5,000$ ft^2) in industrial, commercial, and institutional (called ICI land) land uses, as residential land uses contain relatively few lots, and these lots are usually small.

Sixteen sample boxes were randomly located across Los Angeles. The boxes were large and each contained a mix of land uses. The total area within these boxes was 70,784 acres, or approximately 28.3 percent of the city. The ICI land in the sample boxes equaled 23,742 acres, approximately 34 percent of the city's total ICI land (table 2).

Pan-sharpened QuickBird images were analyzed to separate asphalt surfaces from other impervious surfaces by using ENVI 4.2. Classification results from ENVI were exported to ArcGIS and reclassified into three categories: vegetation cover or no data, parking lot, and nonparking impervious area.

Further processing was required to separate streets from parking areas where trees could be planted. Streets were partitioned from the imagery by overlaying land use shapefiles. Segmentation resulted in delineation of paved parking lot areas, but contained many small polygons representing motor vehicles and other objects within paved parking lot areas. These segments were cleaned up in the ArcGIS environment.

For each council district, the total area of land use type i (*Area_CDLU*, where $i = 3$, industrial, commercial, institutional), the sampled area (*spArea*), and the total area of identified parking lots (*sp_PkArea*) were calculated for each land use. The total paved parking area for land use type i within a council district can be estimated as:

$$CD\_pkArea_i = \frac{sp\_PKArea_i}{spArea_i} \times Area\_CDLU_i$$

Then the total parking lot area for each council district can be calculated as:

$$CD\_pkArea = \sum_i \left(\frac{sp\_PKArea_i}{spArea_i} \times Area\_CDLU_i \right)$$

where $i = 3, 4, 5$.

Table 2—Estimated paved parking lot area by land use and council district

Council district	Land use (ICI)[a]	Total ICI land area	Sampled ICI land area	Paved parking lot area within sampled area	Paved parking lot rate	Estimated paved parking lot area	Total est. paved parking lot area	Paved parking lot rate for ICI land
		Acres	Acres	Acres	Percent	Acres	Acres	Percent
	Ind.	818	575	45	7.9	65		
	Com.	854	692	101	14.5	124		
1	Instit.	1,494	719	25	3.4	51	240	7.6
	Ind.	973	251	45	18.0	175		
	Com.	940	311	93	30.0	282		
2	Instit.	2,049	590	25	4.2	86	544	13.7
	Ind.	731	521	104	20.1	147		
	Com.	1,335	592	175	29.5	394		
3	Instit.	2,240	367	21	5.7	128	669	15.5
	Ind.	402	189	25	13.2	53		
	Com.	997	515	82	15.9	159		
4	Instit.	3,496	411	23	5.6	197	409	8.4
	Ind.	167	100	12	11.6	19		
	Com.	1,077	265	33	12.6	136		
5	Instit.	2,269	223	6	2.8	64	220	6.3
	Ind.	3,362	2,526	302	12.0	402		
	Com.	692	512	160	31.2	216		
6	Instit.	3,633	1,627	78	4.8	174	793	10.3
	Ind.	983	335	105	31.2	307		
	Com.	667	210	71	33.9	226		
7	Instit.	3,080	624	18	3.0	91	624	13.2
	Ind.	179	83	14	16.8	30		
	Com.	980	266	39	14.8	145		
8	Instit.	722	178	21	12.0	87	261	13.9
	Ind.	1,748	461	54	11.8	207		
	Com.	1,043	648	112	17.3	180		
9	Instit.	891	521	50	9.6	85	472	12.8
	Ind.	328	41	2	3.9	13		
	Com.	896	201	26	12.7	114		
10	Instit.	601	138	12	8.7	53	179	9.8
	Ind.	952	499	77	15.4	147		
	Com.	904	319	33	10.3	93		
11	Instit.	3,943	778	51	6.6	260	500	8.6
	Ind.	1,885	1,252	224	17.9	337		
	Com.	972	198	57	28.5	277		
12	Instit.	4,428	483	49	10.1	447	1,061	14.6
	Ind.	412	213	24	11.5	47		
	Com.	950	413	71	17.1	163		
13	Instit.	1,121	554	18	3.2	36	246	9.9
	Ind.	2,113	929	58	6.2	131		
	Com.	708	169	21	12.3	87		
14	Instit.	2,173	641	31	4.9	107	325	6.5
	Ind.	6,815	1,149	264	23.0	1,565		
	Com.	743	252	48	18.9	140		
15	Instit.	3,017	1,199	57	4.8	145	1,850	17.5
Total		70,784	23,742	2,962		8,393		

[a] ICI = industrial (Ind.), commercial (Com.), and institutional (Institut.).

The total parking lot area in a council district is estimated based on the ratio of parking lot area to total area of the same type of land use in the samples summed over land use types. This approach assumes that ratios of parking lot area to land use area found in each council district sample are representative of actual ratios throughout the council district.

To estimate technical PTCC in paved parking areas, the number of potential tree planting sites was assumed to cover 50 percent of the paved area, based on municipal tree shade ordinances that specify 50 percent shade within 10 to 15 years of planting (McPherson 2001). To calculate the number of trees needed to shade 50 percent of the paved area, we assume that all have the 30-ft crown diameter of the medium-stature tree.

Ground-truthing and calibration of PTCC—

The accuracy of potential planting site estimates depends on the accuracy of the initial land cover classification, as well as errors associated with the computer-based tree site selection process. A simple ground-truthing method was applied to estimate the accuracy of identifying potential tree planting sites and to calibrate our findings accordingly.

A stratified random sample of 100 parcels was located across Los Angeles by using the UFORE random plot selection tool (Nowak et al. 2003). The number of sample plots was proportional to area by land use. Personnel from TreePeople visited 55 of the sites to assess the accuracy of computer-generated maps showing potential planting sites for large, medium, and small trees. Sampled parcels were distributed by land use as follows: 44 percent low-density housing, 18 percent medium- to high-density housing, 16 percent industrial, 13 percent commercial, and 9 percent public/open space. Field crews had three maps for each site: aerial photograph (2000, 3-ft resolution, black and white) and two Quickbird pan-sharpened images (2-ft resolution), one showing existing tree cover, the other showing potential tree sites. After locating the property and obtaining permission to conduct the analysis, the crews crossed out potential planting sites that did not exist and drew circles locating sites not identified by the computer program. In some cases, the sizes of trees and their placement were changed in the field by using the same rules that the program applied.

Computer-based estimates of potential tree sites were adjusted by using ratio estimators for each tree size and land use (table 3). Ratio estimators express the ratio of ground-truthed tree sites to computer-generated sites by land use. For example, the value 1.67 for medium trees in the low-density residential land use indicates that the number of plantable sites found from ground truthing was 1.67 times the number generated by the computer.

Overall, the number of ground-truthed potential tree sites was 32 percent less than computer-generated sites, but the overall potential canopy increase was similar (difference is less than 1 percent). This result is explained by the fact that the ground-truthed sites contained relatively more sites for large and medium stature trees than were generated by the computer.

Table 3—Ratio estimators used to correct the number of computer-generated potential tree planting sites based on ground-truthing

| Land use | Tree size | | | | | |
| | Small | | Medium | | Large | |
	Ratio	SE	Ratio	SE	Ratio	SE
Low density residential	0.73	0.72	1.67	1.65	1	1.54
Medium/high-density residential	0.88	0.46	1	0.63	1	0
Industrial	0.28	0.48	0.5	0.8	1.04	0.23
Commercial	0.8	0.49	1.18	0.67	1.62	1.43
Institutional	0.61	0.07	1	0.24	2.2	0.15

SE = standard error.

The computer program generated 877 potential tree planting sites (73 large, 170 medium, and 634 small) that increased TCC by 8.6 acres for the 55 parcels. Our ground-truth results indicated potential for 599 trees (106 large, 158 medium, and 335 small) that increased TCC by 8.7 acres. Overall, the number of ground-truthed potential tree sites was 32 percent less than computer-generated sites, but the overall potential canopy increase was similar (difference is less than 1 percent). This result is explained by the fact that the ground-truthed sites contained relatively more sites for large and medium stature trees than were generated by the computer. After applying the ratio estimators to our computer-generated estimates, the total number of potential sites was reduced.

Tree Canopy Cover Target

The primary purpose behind setting a realistic TCC target for Los Angeles was to determine if the 1-million-tree planting goal was feasible. In the event that our TCC target exceeded the 1-million-tree goal, it would confirm feasibility of the goal and provide impetus for planting in excess of the goal. If our TCC target was less than the goal, it would indicate need to reevaluate the goal.

We examined the distribution of TCC by land use polygons and found that, in most cases, they were not normally distributed. However, determining the appropriate percentile targets for different land uses seemed arbitrary and nonuniform. Therefore, TCC targets for this study were designed to fill 50 percent of the available planting sites in each land use and council district. The exception is for large paved parking lot surfaces (>5,000 ft^2) for commercial and institutional land uses, where we assume that the TCC target is 50 percent of the paved area based on the fact that many municipal parking lot tree shade ordinances have adopted this 50 percent target. However, for industrial land uses we reduced the target to 25 percent TCC because a substantial amount of paved area is used by trucks, as temporary storage, and for loading and unloading. The goal of filling 50 percent of all potential tree planting sites acknowledges that:

- Each council district is unique because it has a different land use mix, as well as different existing and PTCC that reflects historical patterns of development and tree stewardship.

- Every council district can do its "fair share" by filling 50 percent of its available tree planting sites, thus contributing to a shared citywide goal.

- Council districts with the most empty planting sites will achieve the greatest relative increase in TCC, whereas those with higher stocking levels will obtain less enhancement.

The 1-Million-Tree Planting Scenario

The 1-million-tree planting scenario was developed by using the TCC targets and a reduction factor applied uniformly across all council districts and land uses. The reduction factor, 76.5 percent, was the ratio of program trees (1 million) to target trees (1.31 million).

We used existing data on tree benefits for coastal (McPherson et al. 2000) and inland southern California (McPherson et al. 2001) to project future annual benefits from 1 million new trees. Our analysis incorporated a range of mortality rates for typical small, medium, and large growing trees over a 35-year period (2006–2040). Results are reported in terms of annual value per tree planted and cumulative value for the 35-year period. This accounting approach "grows" trees in different locations and uses computer simulation to directly calculate the annual flow of benefits as trees mature and die (McPherson 1992).

Tree Data

Based on discussions with program planners, we assume that 1 million trees are planted during the first 5 years of the program at an increasing rate to allow the program to ramp up as resources and capacity grow:

- 2006–50,000 trees
- 2007–160,000 trees
- 2008–230,000 trees
- 2009–270,000 trees
- 2010–290,000 trees

Low- and high-mortality rates provide realistic bounds for uncertainty regarding survival of transplants. Respective annual mortality rates for establishment (the first 5 years after planting) are 1 percent (low) and 5 percent (high), and thereafter

To account for differences in the growth patterns and benefits of trees of different sizes, we made use of growth curves for small, medium, and large tree species in each climate zone developed from street trees in Santa Monica and Claremont. For the coastal zone, growth curves for the yew, jacaranda, and camphor were used. For the inland zone, growth curves for crapemyrtle, jacaranda, and evergreen ash were used.

rates are 0.5 and 2 percent. Over a 35-year period, these annual mortality rates translate into total low and high rates of about 17 and 56 percent. The average mortality rate is 36.5 percent.

Los Angeles has a variety of climate zones because of its proximity to the Pacific Ocean and the nearby mountain ranges. We have classified each council district as coastal zone or inland zone based on an aggregation of Sunset climate zones (Brenzel 2001). Council districts 11 and 15 are coastal, and the remaining 13 are inland.

To account for differences in the growth patterns and benefits of trees of different sizes, we made use of growth curves for small, medium, and large tree species in each climate zone developed from street trees in Santa Monica and Claremont (McPherson et al. 2000, 2001). For the coastal zone, growth curves for the yew (see "Common and Scientific Names" section), jacaranda, and camphor were used. For the inland zone, growth curves for crapemyrtle, jacaranda, and evergreen ash were used. The mature crown diameters of these species roughly correspond with the 15-, 30-, and 50-ft sizes used in determining potential planting sites. The selection of these species was based on data availability and is not intended to endorse their use in large numbers. In fact, the camphor has a poor form for a street tree and in certain areas crapemyrtle is overused. In addition, relying on too few species can increase the likelihood of catastrophic loss owing to pests, disease, or other threats.

Benefits

Benefits are calculated with numerical models and data for trees in each land use, using methods previously described (McPherson et al. 2000, 2001). Projected energy savings reflect differences in cooling and heating loads associated with coastal and inland zone climates. Similarly, air pollutant uptake calculations use air pollutant concentrations measured at monitoring stations in each zone. Costs of preventing or repairing damage from pollution, flooding, or other environmental risks are used to estimate society's willingness to pay for clean air and water (Wang and Santini 1995). For example, the value of stormwater runoff reduction owing to rainfall interception by trees is estimated by using marginal control costs. If a community or developer is willing to pay an average of $0.01 per gallon of treated and controlled runoff to meet minimum standards, then the stormwater runoff mitigation value of a tree that intercepts 1,000 gal of rain, eliminating the need for control, should be $10.

Energy savings—
Effects of tree shade and urban heat island mitigation on building energy use are applied to trees planted in residential areas only. Energy effects were based on

computer simulations that incorporated building, climate, and shading effects (McPherson and Simpson 1999). Tree distribution with respect to residential buildings was determined by classifying 130 potential planting sites in 34 ground-truthed low-density housing parcels by azimuth and distance class from the building (table 4). We lack sufficient data on nonresidential building stock and tree location effects to simulate energy savings for these buildings.

Typical meteorological year weather data for Los Angeles International Airport (coastal) and Riverside (inland), as well as local building characteristics were used. The dollar values of electrical energy ($0.10634 per kWh) and natural gas ($0.0067 per kBtu) were based on retail residential electricity and natural gas prices obtained from the Los Angeles Department of Water and Power (LADWP).

Atmospheric carbon dioxide reductions—

Sequestration, the net rate of carbon dioxide (CO_2) storage in above- and below-ground biomass over the course of one growing season, was calculated by using Santa Monica (coastal) and Claremont (inland) tree growth data and biomass equations for urban trees (Pillsbury et al. 1998). The CO_2 released through decomposition of dead woody biomass was based on annual tree removal rates. The CO_2 released during tree maintenance activities was estimated based on annual consumption of gasoline and diesel fuel as 0.635 lb per in of diameter at breast height (d.b.h.), the average of values previously used (McPherson et al. 2000, 2001).

Reductions in building energy use result in reduced emissions of CO_2. Emission reductions were calculated as the product of energy savings and CO_2 emission factors for electricity and heating. Heating fuel was natural gas, and the fuel mix for electrical generation was 52 percent coal, 6 percent hydro, 26 percent natural gas, 11 percent nuclear, and 5 percent other. The value of CO_2 reductions was $6.68 per ton of CO_2 (Pearce 2003).

Air quality benefits–

The hourly pollutant dry deposition per tree was expressed as the product of deposition velocity $V_d = 1/(R_a+R_b+R_c)$ (where R_a, R_b, and R_c are aerodynamic, boundary layer, and stomatal resistances), pollutant concentration C, canopy projection area (CPA), and a time step. Hourly deposition velocities for ozone (O_3), nitrogen dioxide

Table 4—Distribution of potential tree planting sites around homes based on ground-truthing

Distance classes	North	Northeast	East	Southeast	South	Southwest	West	Northwest
				Percent				
Adjacent (<20 ft)	10.8	1.5	10.0	2.3	10.0	3.8	6.2	2.3
Near (21 to 40 ft)	7.7	2.3	12.3	4.6	6.2	3.8	3.8	1.5
Far (41 to 60 ft)	1.5	0.0	3.8	1.5	1.5	0.8	0.8	0.8

(NO_2), sulfur dioxide (SO_2), and particulate matter of <10-micron diameter (PM_{10}) were calculated by using estimates for the resistances R_a, R_b, and R_c for each hour throughout a "base year" (Scott et al. 1998). Hourly meteorological data and pollutant concentrations were obtained from monitoring stations in Hawthorne (coastal) and Azusa (inland) when pollutant concentrations were near average.

Energy savings result in reduced emissions of criteria air pollutants (volatile organic hydrocarbons [VOCs], NO_2, SO_2, PM_{10}) from power plants and space-heating equipment. These avoided emissions were calculated by using LADWP emission factors for electricity and heating fuels.

Emissions of biogenic volatile organic compounds (BVOCs) from trees affect O_3 formation. The hourly emission rates of the four tree species used in this analysis are minimal (Benjamin and Winer 1998). In reality, a large-scale tree planting like this is likely to include some species with emission rates higher than reported here. Although our approach may understate BVOC emissions from new trees, it also understates the air quality benefit associated with lowered summertime air temperatures and the resulting reduced hydrocarbon emissions from anthropogenic and biogenic sources.

The monetary value of tree effects on air quality should reflect the value that society places on clean air, as indicated by willingness to pay for pollutant reductions. Lacking specific data for Los Angeles, air quality benefits were monetized as damage values (table 5) by using regression relationships among emission values, pollutant concentrations, and population numbers (Wang and Santini 1995). This regression provides estimates of the costs of damages to human health resulting from air pollution.

Stormwater runoff reductions—
A numerical interception model accounted for the amount of annual rainfall intercepted by trees, as well as throughfall and stem flow (Xiao et al. 2000). The volume of water stored in tree crowns was calculated from tree crown leaf and stem surface areas and water depth on these surfaces. Hourly meteorological and rainfall data for

Table 5—Values of air pollutant reduction for coastal and inland zones

Pollutant	Coastal	Inland
	Dollars per pound	
Nitrogen dioxide	2.26	3.95
Sulfur dioxide	2.50	2.50
Small particulate matter	5.44	4.95
Volatile organic compounds	1.06	1.98
Ozone	2.26	3.95

1996 from California Irrigation Management Information System stations in Santa Monica and Claremont were used because total rainfall in that year was close to the average annual amount.

Stormwater runoff reduction benefits were priced by estimating costs of controlling stormwater runoff and treating sanitary waste in Los Angeles. During small rainfall events, excess capacity in sanitary treatment plants can be used to treat stormwater. In the Los Angeles region, it costs approximately $0.0018 per gal to treat sanitary waste (Condon and Moriarty 1999). We used this price to value the water quality benefit of rainfall interception by trees because the cost of treating stormwater in central facilities is likely to be close to the cost of treating an equal amount of sanitary waste.

To calculate water quality benefit, the treatment cost is multiplied by gallons of rainfall intercepted after the first 0.1 in has fallen for each event (24 hours without rain) during the year. The first 0.1 in of rainfall seldom results in runoff, and thus, interception is not a benefit until precipitation exceeds this amount. Over $50 million ($500,000 per square mile) is spent annually controlling floods in the Los Angeles area (Condon and Moriarty 1999). We assume that rainfall interception by tree crowns will have minimal effect during very large storms that result in cata-strophic flooding of the Los Angeles River and its tributaries (133-year storm).

Although storm drains are designed to control 25-year events, localized flooding is a problem during smaller events. We assume that $50 million is spent per year for local problem areas, and the annual value of peak flow reduction is $500,000 per square mile for each 25-year peak flow event (Jones & Stokes Associates, Inc. 1998). A 25-year winter event deposits 6.7 in of rainfall during 67 hours. Approximately $0.0054 per gal is spent annually for controlling flooding caused by such an event. Water quality and flood control benefits are summed to calculate the total hydrology benefit of $0.0072 per gal. This price is multiplied by the amount of rainfall intercepted annually, after excluding events less than 0.1 in.

Aesthetics and other benefits—

Many benefits attributed to urban trees are difficult to price (e.g., beautification, privacy, wildlife habitat, sense of place, well-being). However, the value of some of these benefits can be captured in the differences in sales prices of properties with and without trees. Anderson and Cordell (1988) found that each large front-yard tree in Athens, Georgia, was associated with a 0.88-percent increase in sales price. In this analysis, aesthetic (A) benefits (dollars per tree per year) are expressed for a single tree as:

$$A = L \times P$$

where L is the annual increase in tree leaf area (LA) and P is the adjusted price (dollars per square foot of LA) :

$$P = (T \times C) / M$$

where

T = Large tree contribution to home sales price = 0.88 percent × median sales price

C = Tree location factor (percent) that discounts the benefit for trees outside of low-density residential areas

M = Large tree LA

The median sales price for single-family homes in Los Angeles in December 2006 was $530,000 (California Association of Realtors 2006). The values for C were 100 percent for low-density residential, 70 percent for medium/high-density residential, and 40 percent for other land uses (Gonzales 2004, McPherson 2001). The values for M were 2,691 and 3,591 ft^2 for coastal and inland zones, respectively.

Results

Existing Tree Canopy Cover

The TCC in the city of Los Angeles is 21 percent (52,493 acres) (table 6). Irrigated grass and dry grass/bare soil account for 12 percent (31,206 acres) and 6 percent (13,790 acres) of the city, respectively (fig. 4). Impervious (e.g., paving, roofs) and

Table 6—Land cover distribution by council district (excludes mountains) for Los Angeles

Council district	Land area	Tree canopy cover		Irrigated grass cover		Dry grass /bare soil		Impervious/other		Mountain
	Acres	Acres	Percent	Acres	Percent	Acres	Percent	Acres	Percent	Acres
1	7,949	1,266	15.9	474	6.00	395	5.00	5,814	73.0	873
2	20,295	5,395	26.6	1,987	9.80	1,310	6.50	11,603	57.0	11,489
3	24,359	6,345	26.0	3,443	14.10	1,458	6.00	13,114	54.0	2,076
4	15,403	4,429	28.8	1,954	12.70	679	4.40	8,341	54.0	4,069
5	24,317	9,047	37.2	2,798	11.50	737	3.00	11,735	48.0	5,842
6	17,047	2,550	15.0	1,808	10.60	945	5.50	11,744	69.0	-
7	15,789	2,572	16.3	1,513	9.60	2,334	14.80	9,371	59.0	2,540
8	11,174	1,192	10.7	2,175	19.50	414	3.70	7,393	66.0	-
9	9,564	719	7.5	838	8.80	254	2.70	7,753	81.0	-
10	8,541	1,018	11.9	812	9.50	415	4.90	6,296	74.0	-
11	25,922	6,094	23.5	4,467	17.20	642	2.50	14,719	57.0	15,259
12	29,232	5,796	19.8	4,751	16.30	2,258	7.70	16,426	56.0	7,060
13	7,845	1,072	13.7	889	11.30	323	4.10	5,560	71.0	72
14	13,972	3,126	22.4	673	4.80	704	5.00	9,470	68.0	928
15	20,976	1,871	8.9	2,625	12.50	923	4.40	15,557	74.0	-
Total	252,384	52,493	20.8	31,206	12.40	13,790	5.50	154,895	61.0	50,208

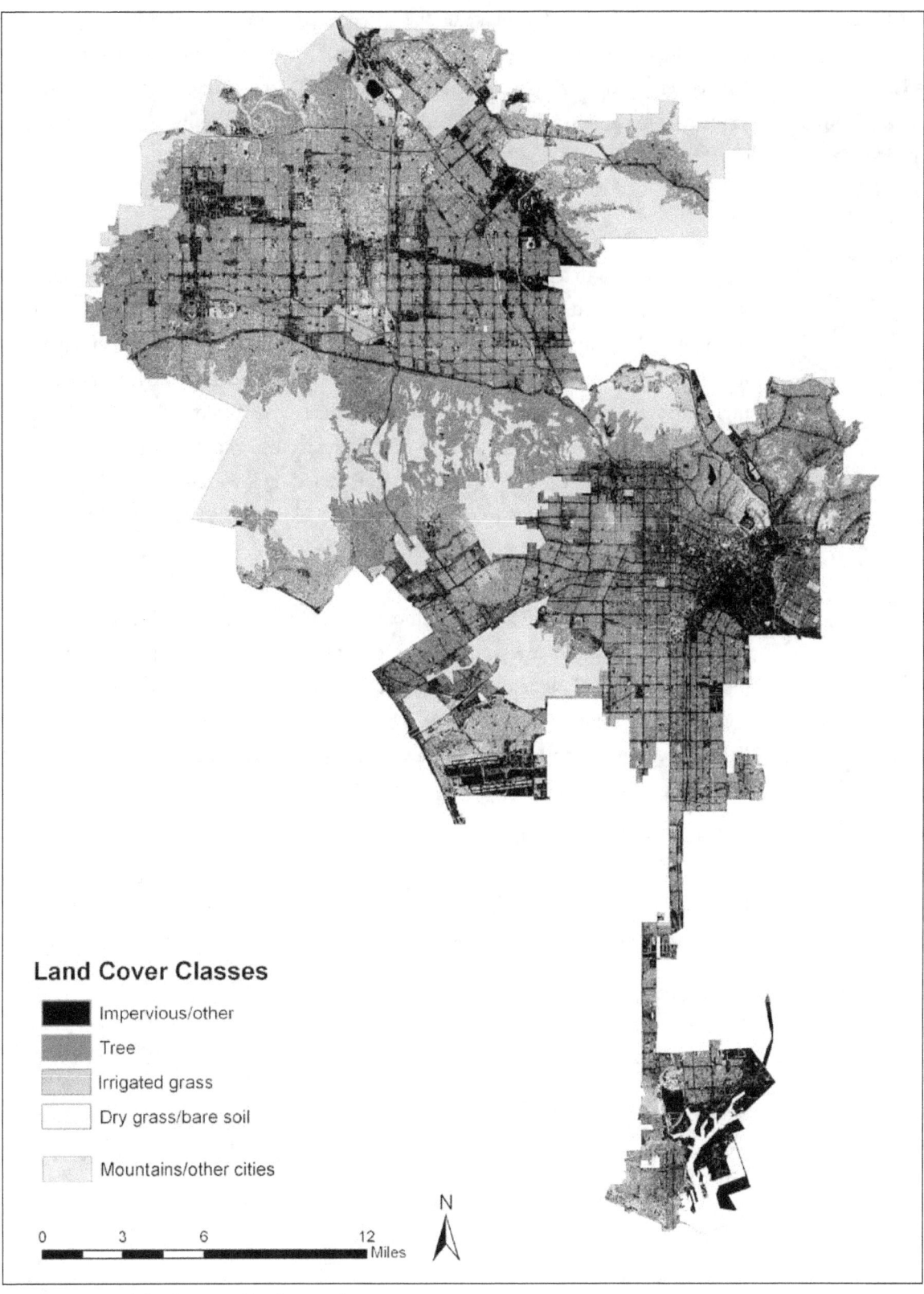

Land Cover Classes

- Impervious/other
- Tree
- Irrigated grass
- Dry grass/bare soil
- Mountains/other cities

0   3   6   12 Miles

N

Figure 4—Spatial distribution of land cover classes.

One-third of Los Angeles's land cover is existing TCC and grass/bare soil with potential to become TCC. The number of existing trees is estimated to be 10.8 million assuming an average tree crown diameter of 16.4 ft.

other surfaces (i.e., water) make up the remaining 61 percent (154,895 acres) of the city's land cover (excluding mountainous areas). Hence, one-third of Los Angeles's land cover is existing TCC and grass/bare soil with potential to become TCC. The number of existing trees is estimated to be 10.8 million assuming an average tree crown diameter of 16.4 ft.

By council district—

At the council district level, TCC ranged from lows of 7 to 9 percent in council districts 9 and 15 to a high of 37 percent in council district 5 (table 6). The TCC was strongly related to land use. As expected, low-density residential land uses had the highest TCC citywide (31 percent), whereas industrial and commercial land uses had the lowest TCC (3 and 6 percent) (table 7). Tree canopy cover tended to be higher in areas near mountains compared to areas closer to downtown Los Angeles.

Relations between TCC and land use are evident in council districts 5 and 9. Council district 5 (37 percent TCC) is dominated by low-density housing (70 percent) and has 49 percent tree/grass/soil cover. In contrast, low-density housing covered only 4 percent of council district 9 (7 percent TCC), whereas industrial and commercial land uses covered 42 percent of the land (table 8).

There are approximately 10.8 million trees (43 trees per acre) in Los Angeles. Council districts estimated to have the highest tree densities are 5 (37 percent), 4 (29 percent), 2 (27 percent), and 3 (26 percent) (fig. 5). These council districts contain approximately 77, 59, 55, and 53 trees per acre, respectively. Council districts with the lowest estimated tree densities are 9 (8 percent), 15 (9 percent), 8 (11 percent), and 10 (12 percent).

By neighborhood council—

The TCC and area are presented for each of the 86 neighborhood councils in the appendix. Existing TCC exceeded 40 percent in three neighborhood councils: Bel Air-Beverly Crest (53 percent), Arroyo Seco (46 percent), and Studio City (42

Table 7—Land cover distribution by land use

Land use	Total area	Tree cover		Grass cover		Dry grass /bare soil	
	Acres	*Acres*	*Percent*	*Acres*	*Percent*	*Acres*	*Percent*
Low-density residential	120,151	36,615	30.5	18,182	15.1	8,601	7.2
Medium/high-density residential	43,803	6,351	14.5	4,377	10.0	1,881	4.3
Industrial	25,693	901	3.5	649	2.5	493	1.9
Commercial	20,130	1,121	5.6	622	3.1	352	1.7
Institutional	39,093	7,174	18.3	6,809	17.4	2,356	6.0
Unknown	3,514	331	9.4	566	16.2	107	3.1
Total	252,384	52,493	20.8	31,206	12.4	13,790	5.5

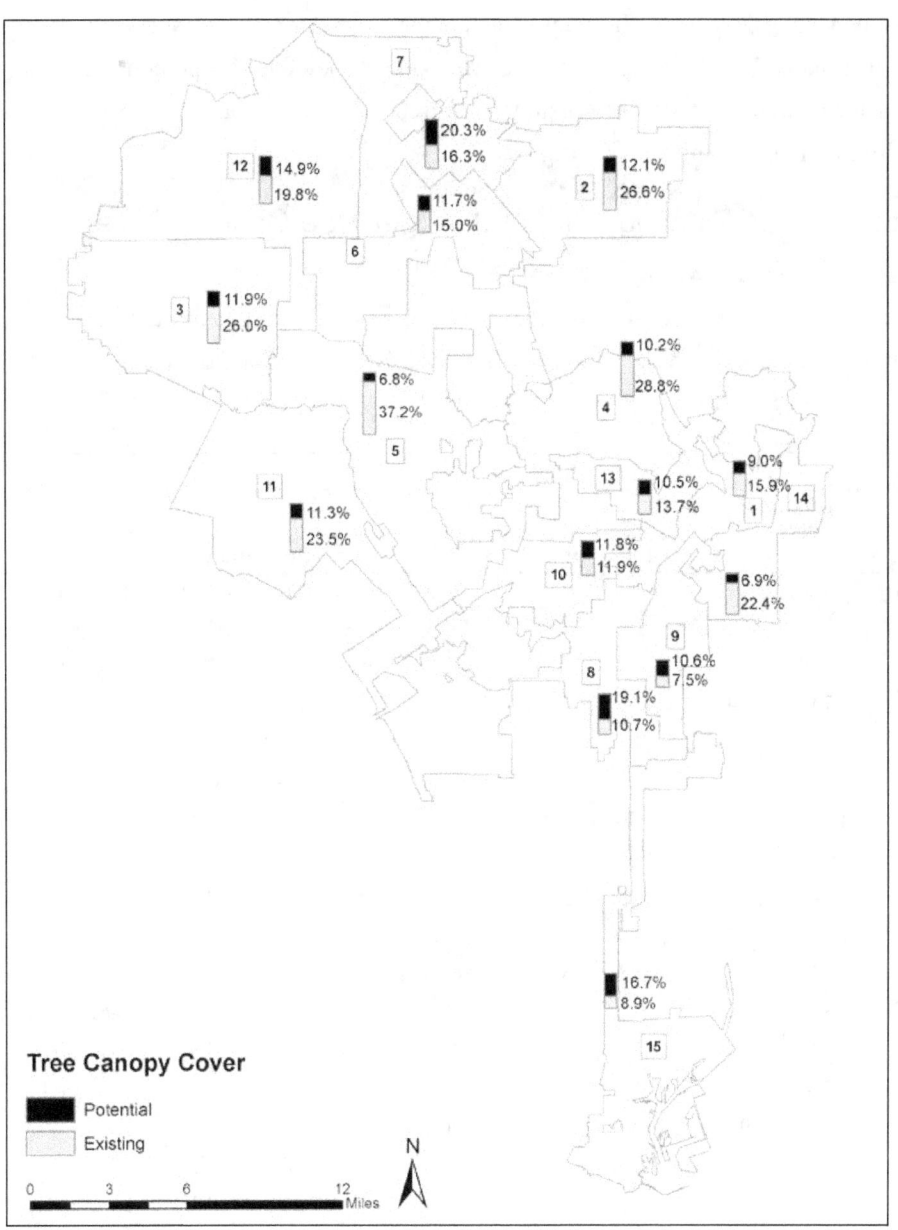

Figure 5—Existing and potential tree canopy cover by council district.

We estimate that there are approximately 2.47 million potential tree planting sites. If all potential tree sites were filled and the canopy matured, TCC would increase to 33 percent from 21 percent.

percent). Neighborhood councils with the lowest TCC were Downtown Los Angeles (3 percent), Wilmington (5 percent), and Historic Cultural and Macarthur (6 percent). The mean TCC was 17.7 percent and standard deviation was 9.8 percent.

Accuracy assessment—
Overall classification accuracy was 88.6 percent based on the pixel-by-pixel comparison. The accuracy for classifying existing TCC was 74.3 percent (table 9). Not surprisingly, TCC was most often misclassified as irrigated grass (13 percent),

and vice versa (17 percent). In the parcel-scale analysis, impervious surface was underestimated by 3.5 percent and TCC was overestimated by 5.0 percent. Factors that affected mapping accuracy included the treatment of the shadowed area and minimum mapping units during digitizing.

Potential Tree Planting Sites and Target Tree Canopy Cover

Potential tree planting sites—

After calibrating computer-estimated potential tree sites with ground-truthed data, we estimate that there are approximately 2.47 million potential tree planting

Table 8—Land use distribution by council district

Council District	Total area	Land use											
		Low-density residential		Medium/high-density residential		Industrial		Commercial		Institutional		Unknown	
		Acres	Percent	Acres	Percent	Acres	Percent	Acres	Percent	Acres	Percent	Acres	Percent
1	7,949	1,117	14.1	2,751	34.6	1,017	12.8	1,299	16.3	1,763	22.2		
2	20,295	12,760	62.9	2,798	13.8	1,113	5.5	1,323	6.5	2,294	11.3	8	0.04
3	24,359	17,486	71.8	1,736	7.1	846	3.5	1,754	7.2	2,537	10.4		
4	15,403	6,374	41.4	3,378	21.9	482	3.1	1,460	9.5	3,709	24.1		
5	24,317	17,094	70.3	2,878	11.8	215	0.9	1,638	6.7	2,488	10.2	4	0.02
6	17,047	6,723	39.4	1,616	9.5	3,776	22.2	934	5.5	3,997	23.4	1	0.01
7	15,789	8,550	54.2	1,907	12.1	1,121	7.1	879	5.6	3,332	21.1		
8	11,174	4,750	42.5	3,725	33.3	235	2.1	1,604	14.4	860	7.7		
9	9,564	339	3.5	4,084	42.7	2,389	25.0	1,639	17.1	1,113	11.6		
10	8,541	1,841	21.6	4,142	48.5	465	5.4	1,361	15.9	731	8.6		
11	25,922	12,004	46.3	3,502	13.5	1,170	4.5	1,377	5.3	4,373	16.9	3,496	13.49
12	29,232	19,595	67.0	1,422	4.9	2,177	7.4	1,224	4.2	4,813	16.5	1	0.01
13	7,845	1,110	14.2	3,526	44.9	504	6.4	1,439	18.3	1,265	16.1	1	0.01
14	13,972	5,053	36.2	2,711	19.4	2,635	18.9	1,090	7.8	2,483	17.8		
15	20,976	5,356	25.5	3,627	17.3	7,547	36.0	1,109	5.3	3,335	15.9	2	0.01
Total	252,384	120,151	47.6	43,803	17.4	25,693	10.2	20,130	8.0	39,093	15.5	3,514	1.39

Table 9—Land cover classification error matrix (number and percentage of pixels correctly identified) for four classes[a]

		Classification								
		Number of pixels					Percent			
		TCC	IG	S	IP	Total	TCC	IG	S	IP
	TCC	**145,335**	25,451	2,871	21,905	195,562	**74.3**	13	1.5	11.2
	IG	17,290	**65,188**	5,989	11,369	99,836	17.3	**65.3**	6	11.4
Base map	S	1,402	1,435	**2,717**	4,795	10,349	13.5	13.9	**26.3**	46.3
	IP	41,290	17,737	21,258	**1,134,016**	1,214,301	3.4	1.5	1.8	**93.4**
	Total	205,317	109,811	32,835	1,172,085	1,520,048	13.5	7.2	2.2	77.1

TC = tree cover, IG = irrigated grass, S = soil, IP-impervious
[a] Rows show the distribution of the class in the base map, columns show the distribution in quickbird pixels The overall accuracy for all classes is 88 6 percent

Table 10—Existing and target tree canopy cover (TCC) and potential and additional tree numbers and TCC by council district and mature tree size class

Council district	Area	Existing TCC		Potential trees				Potential TCC		Additional trees				Additional TCC		Target TCC
	Acres	Acres	Percent	Small	Medium	Large	Total	Acres	Percent	Small	Medium	Large	Total	Acres	Percent	Percent
1	7,949	1,266	15.9	23,821	18,320	7,087	49,228	713	9.0	11,910	11,856	3,543	27,310	400	5.0	21.0
2	20,295	5,395	26.6	109,200	78,161	16,590	203,950	2,459	12.1	54,600	44,750	8,295	107,645	1,322	6.5	33.1
3	24,359	6,345	26.0	144,751	89,421	18,905	253,078	2,890	11.9	72,376	52,755	9,453	134,583	1,576	6.5	32.5
4	15,403	4,429	28.8	70,179	45,282	12,265	127,726	1,572	10.2	35,090	28,126	6,133	69,348	875	5.7	34.4
5	24,317	9,047	37.2	107,119	52,056	8,465	167,640	1,661	6.8	53,560	29,120	4,232	86,912	881	3.6	40.8
6	17,047	2,550	15.0	66,538	64,545	15,175	146,258	2,001	11.7	33,269	38,289	7,587	79,145	1,098	6.4	21.4
7	15,789	2,572	16.3	116,529	86,463	29,355	232,347	3,199	20.3	58,264	48,120	14,678	121,062	1,679	10.6	26.9
8	11,174	1,192	10.7	84,116	61,943	17,577	163,637	2,139	19.1	42,058	34,534	8,788	85,380	1,127	10.1	20.8
9	9,564	719	7.5	40,970	31,665	7,481	80,115	1,017	10.6	20,485	19,925	3,740	44,150	575	6.0	13.5
10	8,541	1,018	11.9	47,971	27,641	8,037	83,649	1,005	11.8	23,986	16,389	4,018	44,393	544	6.4	18.3
11	25,922	6,094	23.5	132,350	84,742	22,527	239,619	2,927	11.3	66,175	47,814	11,264	125,253	1,552	6.0	29.5
12	29,232	5,796	19.8	180,791	127,648	34,104	342,543	4,342	14.9	90,396	74,985	17,052	182,433	2,352	8.0	27.9
13	7,845	1,072	13.7	37,459	24,539	6,150	68,148	827	10.5	18,730	15,331	3,075	37,135	463	5.9	19.6
14	13,972	3,126	22.4	39,821	29,272	7,244	76,337	963	6.9	19,911	17,627	3,622	41,159	530	3.8	26.2
15	20,976	1,871	8.9	90,963	116,363	27,585	234,912	3,501	16.7	45,482	62,570	13,793	121,844	1,822	8.7	17.6
Total	252,384	52,493	20.8	1,292,578	938,062	238,546	2,469,186	31,219	12.4	646,289	542,192	119,273	1,307,754	16,797	6.7	27.5

sites in Los Angeles (table 10). This potential for new trees covers 31,219 acres, or 12 percent of the city. Hence, if all potential tree sites were filled and the canopy matured as noted above, TCC would increase to 33 percent from 21 percent. Fifty-two percent of these potential sites are for small trees (15-ft crown diameter at maturity), 38 percent for medium trees (30-ft at maturity), and 10 percent for large trees (50 ft). All potential parking lot tree sites, which are estimated to equal 258,642 (10.5 percent), are assumed to be for medium trees, although in reality there will be a mix of tree sizes.

The distribution of potential tree sites differs by land use. Low-density residential areas contain the largest number of potential sites (1.4 million, 58 percent), followed by institutional (377,574, 15 percent) and medium/high-density residential (360,382, 15 percent). Industrial and commercial land uses each contain about 6 percent (about 140,000) of the total potential tree planting sites.

Six council districts (2, 3, 7, 11, 12, and 15) have potential for over 200,000 new trees, with these trees adding an additional 11 to 20 percent TCC when mature and assuming no mortality (table 10). Five council districts (1, 9, 10, 13, and 14) have space for fewer than 100,000 trees, with potential to increase TCC by 7 to 12 percent (fig. 5).

Target tree canopy cover–

The target TCC for Los Angeles accounts for the fact that only about 50 percent of the potential sites are suitable for planting owing to residents' desire for no additional trees and conflicts with higher priority uses. Thus, it is realistic for Los Angeles to strive to increase its TCC by 6.7 percent (16,797 acres), which equates to 1.3 million tree sites (table 10). If all additional tree sites were filled and the canopy matured as noted above, TCC would increase to 28 percent from 21 percent. This finding indicates that the goal of planting 1 million trees is feasible.

The distribution of additional tree sites among size classes and land uses is similar to the distribution of potential sites described above. Most sites are for small and medium trees (49 percent and 42 percent). Over 70 percent of the target tree sites are located in low-density residential and institutional land uses. About 16 percent (202,482) of the sites are in large parking lots.

Filling additional tree sites in council districts with the least TCC would increase relative TCC the most (table 10). For example, TCC would increase by 9 to 10 percent in council districts 8 (from 10.7 to 20.8 percent) and 15 (from 8.9 to 17.6 percent) (fig. 6). Similarly, the relative increase would be least in council districts with the greatest TCC, for example, a 3.5-percent increase in council district 5 (from 37.2 to 40.8 percent). If the targeted TCC were filled with 1.3 million trees, TCC would range from 13 to 40 percent across council districts, instead of the current 8 to 37 percent.

In summary, the existing TCC of Los Angeles is 20.8 percent, comprising approximately 10.8 million trees (table 11). There is potential to add 2.5 million additional trees or 12.4 percent TCC. Thus, technical potential for Los Angeles is 33.2 percent TCC or about 13.3 million trees. However, it is not realistic to think that every possible tree site will be planted. Assuming that about 50 percent of

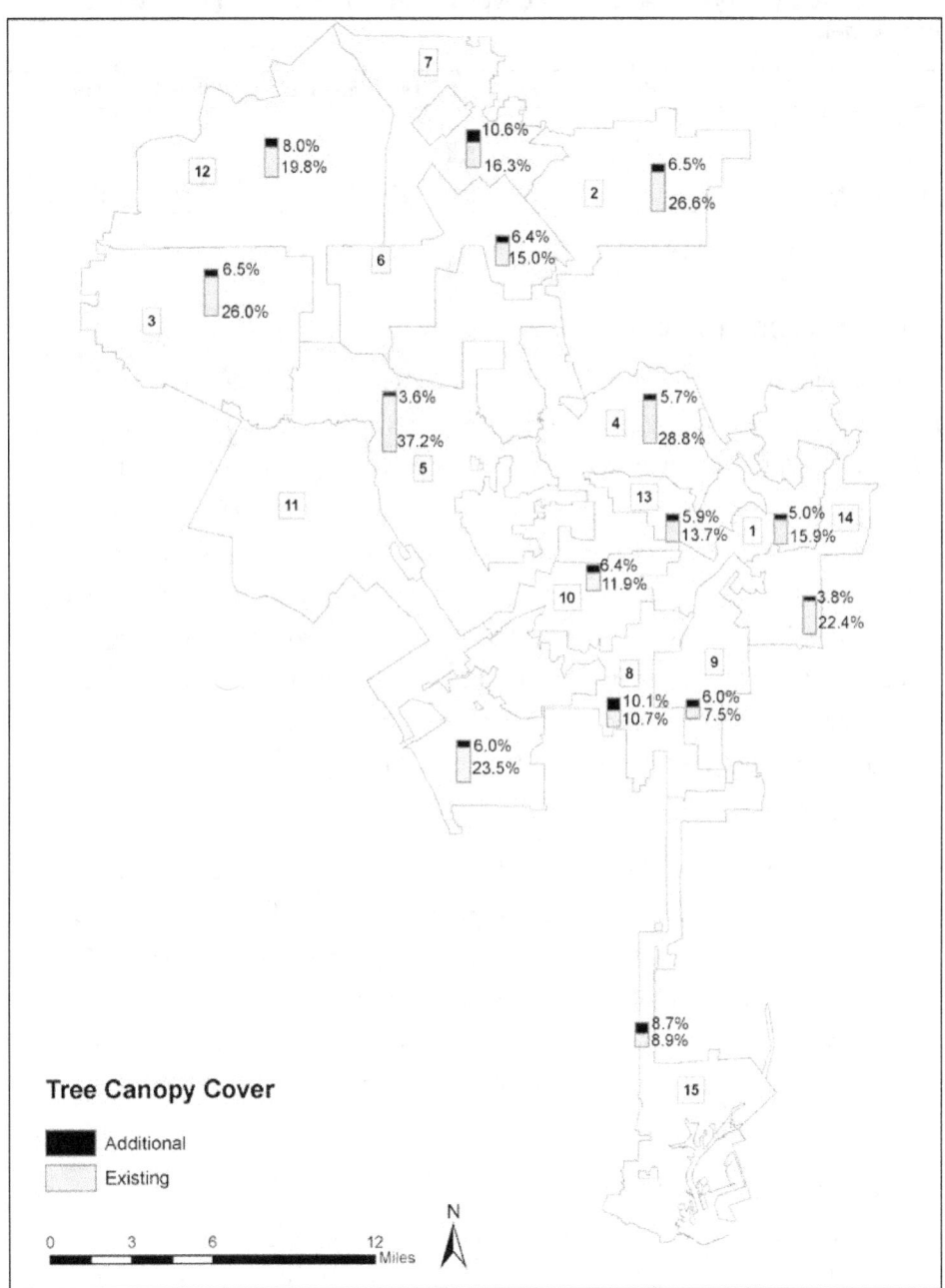

Figure 6—Existing and target tree canopy cover by council district.

the unplanted sites are feasible to plant results in adding 1.3 million more trees equivalent to a 6.7 percent increase in TCC. Hence, market potential (target TCC) is 27.5 percent of TCC or 12.1 million trees. Planting 1 million trees is feasible, and, if accomplished as indicated above, would saturate 97 percent of the existing market potential.

Table 11—Summary of tree canopy cover and tree number estimates for Los Angeles

	Existing	Potential	Tech potential	Additional	Target
Tree canopy cover (percent)	20.8	12.4	33.2	6.7	27.5
Tree numbers	10,824,628	2,469,186	13,293,814	1,307,754	12,132,382

Benefits From 1 Million Trees

Benefits forecast from the planting of 1 million trees in Los Angeles depend on tree mortality, as well as climate zone, land use, and tree species. Our planting scenarios reflect effects of low (17 percent) and high (56 percent) mortality rates on tree numbers and associated benefits. After 35 years (2040), the number of surviving trees equals 828,924 and 444,889 for the low- and high-mortality scenarios, respectively. In both scenarios, the 1-million planted trees are distributed among council districts (fig. 7) and land uses such that 55 percent are in low-density residential, 17 percent in institutional, 14 percent in medium/high-density residential, 9 percent in commercial, and 5 percent in industrial. Nearly one-half of the trees are small (49 percent), 42 percent are medium, and 9 percent are large at maturity.

Citywide benefits—
Benefits calculated annually and totaled for the 35-year period are $1.33 and $1.95 billion for the high- and low-mortality scenarios, respectively (tables 12 and 13). These values translate into $1,328 and $1,951 per tree planted, or $38 and $56 per tree per year when divided by the 35-year period.

Eighty-one percent of total benefits are aesthetic/other, 8 percent are stormwater runoff reduction, 6 percent energy savings, 4 percent air quality improvement, and less than 1 percent atmospheric carbon reduction (fig. 8).

Benefits by land use and council district—
The distribution of benefits among council districts is closely related to the climate zone and the number of trees. Benefits per tree are about 50 percent less ($700 to 1,000 instead of $1,300 to 2,400) in the coastal zone (council districts 11 and

Another factor influencing the distribution of benefits among council districts is the mix of land uses. Districts with relatively less land for housing and relatively more land for commercial, industrial, and institutional use have lower benefits per tree planted.

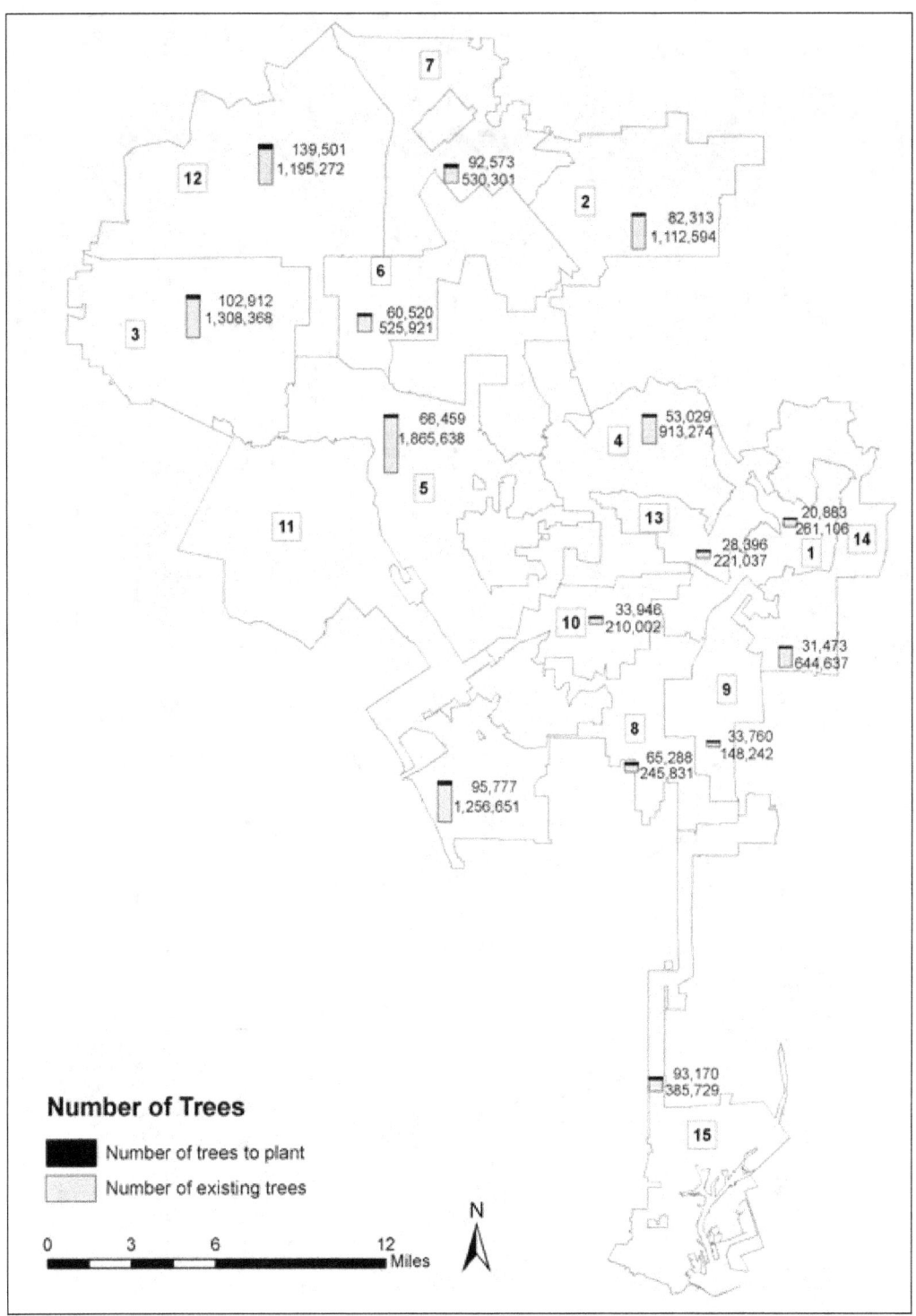

Figure 7—Number of existing trees and trees to plant (1 million total) by council district.

Table 12—Cumulative benefits (2006–2040) and average benefit per tree planted by council district for the low-mortality scenario

Council district	Trees planted	Trees alive in 2040	Energy		Air quality		Carbon dioxide		Runoff		Aesthetic/other		Total benefits	
			Dollars	Dollars per tree	Dollars	Dollars per tree	Dollars	Dollars per tree	Dollars	Dollars per tree	Dollars	Dollars per tree	Dollars	Dollars per tree
1	20,883	17,311	1,415,847	68	1,762,961	84	162,689	8	3,950,229	189	31,278,375	1,498	38,570,101	1,847
2	82,313	68,231	12,974,614	158	7,850,324	95	859,878	10	14,621,169	178	156,354,878	1,900	192,660,864	2,341
3	102,912	85,306	15,351,113	149	9,400,287	91	1,013,258	10	17,362,590	169	181,878,208	1,767	225,005,456	2,186
4	53,029	43,957	5,549,222	105	4,536,519	86	443,172	8	9,291,042	175	82,645,520	1,559	102,465,473	1,932
5	66,459	55,090	10,213,205	154	5,708,874	86	622,241	9	9,757,767	147	109,185,934	1,643	135,488,021	2,039
6	60,520	50,167	6,845,792	113	5,679,725	94	553,869	9	12,293,102	203	105,723,228	1,747	131,095,715	2,166
7	92,573	76,736	13,470,678	146	8,848,116	96	1,007,167	11	16,254,404	176	177,691,502	1,919	217,271,868	2,347
8	65,288	54,119	10,358,233	159	6,331,353	97	721,359	11	11,505,944	176	131,054,146	2,007	159,971,035	2,450
9	33,760	27,984	2,330,587	69	2,768,387	82	231,661	7	6,439,504	191	47,375,894	1,403	59,146,034	1,752
10	33,946	28,139	4,063,135	120	2,911,931	86	303,757	9	5,524,913	163	55,755,710	1,642	68,559,446	2,020
11	95,777	79,392	4,494,173	47	4,561,895	48	319,986	3	5,135,221	54	77,801,510	812	92,312,785	964
12	139,501	115,635	20,486,019	147	13,172,516	94	1,442,660	10	24,774,501	178	259,540,968	1,860	319,416,665	2,290
13	28,396	23,538	2,530,265	89	2,347,087	83	214,871	8	5,031,419	177	42,054,322	1,481	52,177,964	1,837
14	31,473	26,089	3,444,288	109	2,774,938	88	271,603	9	5,761,254	183	51,541,911	1,638	63,793,994	2,027
15	93,170	77,231	3,895,333	42	4,755,920	51	309,052	3	5,382,414	58	78,262,865	840	92,605,585	994
Total	1,000,000	828,924	117,422,505	117	83,410,834	83	8,477,224	8	153,085,472	153	1,588,144,972	1,588	1,950,541,007	1,951

Table 13—Cumulative benefits (2006–2040) and average benefit per tree planted by council district for the high-mortality scenario

Council district	Trees planted	Trees alive in 2040	Energy		Air quality		Carbon dioxide		Runoff		Aesthetic/other		Total benefits	
			Dollars	Dollars per tree	Dollars	Dollars per tree	Dollars	Dollars per tree	Dollars	Dollars per tree	Dollars	Dollars per tree	Dollars	Dollars per tree
1	20,883	9,291	912,296	44	1,121,764	54	94,218	4.51	2,511,415	120.26	21,507,152	1,030	26,146,845	1,252
2	82,313	36,620	8,367,563	102	5,008,384	61	522,874	6.35	9,295,655	112.93	107,544,314	1,307	130,738,789	1,588
3	102,912	45,784	9,900,006	96	5,996,296	58	616,283	5.99	11,037,937	107.26	124,949,646	1,214	152,500,169	1,482
4	53,029	23,592	3,578,062	67	2,890,179	55	264,175	4.98	5,906,717	111.39	56,805,841	1,071	69,444,974	1,310
5	66,459	29,567	6,586,022	99	3,642,382	55	381,817	5.75	6,202,337	93.33	74,881,653	1,127	91,694,211	1,380
6	60,520	26,925	4,415,479	73	3,619,609	60	329,891	5.45	7,816,601	129.16	72,874,493	1,204	89,056,074	1,472
7	92,573	41,185	8,687,081	94	5,642,314	61	605,258	6.54	10,333,083	111.62	122,123,766	1,319	147,391,503	1,592
8	65,288	29,046	6,678,559	102	4,038,655	62	436,477	6.69	7,314,704	112.04	90,137,473	1,381	108,605,867	1,663
9	33,760	15,019	1,500,722	44	1,761,633	52	135,277	4.01	4,094,339	121.28	32,600,171	966	40,092,141	1,188
10	33,946	15,102	2,618,321	77	1,855,579	55	182,259	5.37	3,512,055	103.46	38,273,115	1,127	46,441,329	1,368
11	95,777	42,610	2,921,106	30	2,966,367	31	190,585	1.99	3,320,115	34.67	55,843,968	583	65,242,141	681
12	139,501	62,062	13,211,419	95	8,401,166	60	871,748	6.25	15,750,370	112.91	178,387,854	1,279	216,622,557	1,553
13	28,396	12,633	1,630,553	57	1,494,522	53	127,237	4.48	3,198,768	112.65	28,920,459	1,018	35,371,539	1,246
14	31,473	14,002	2,220,566	71	1,768,095	56	162,091	5.15	3,662,890	116.38	35,447,144	1,126	43,260,785	1,375
15	93,170	41,451	2,521,639	27	3,091,410	33	181,931	1.95	3,477,891	37.33	55,895,029	600	65,167,901	699
Total	1,000,000	444,889	75,749,392	76	53,298,356	53	5,102,121	5.10	97,434,876	97.43	1,096,192,081	1,096	1,327,776,826	1,328

15) than the inland zone because the growth curve data indicate that the trees are smaller, air pollutant concentrations are lower, and building heating and cooling loads are less because of the milder climate (figs. 9 and 10).

Another factor influencing the distribution of benefits among council districts is the mix of land uses (fig. 11). Districts with relatively less land for housing and relatively more land for commercial, industrial, and institutional use have lower benefits per tree planted. Energy savings are less because our model did not estimate benefits for heating and cooling effects in nonresidential buildings. Our model did not incorporate effects of trees on cooling and heating of nonresidential buildings. For example, residential land uses occupied only 35 to 37 percent of the land in council districts 1 and 9, and average benefits were among the lowest per tree (about $1,800 and $1,200 for low- and high-mortality scenarios) for all inland council districts. On the other hand, in council districts 2, 7, and 8, residential land uses exceeded 52 percent of total land, and average benefits were the highest (greater than $2,300 per tree for the low-mortality scenario).

Citywide Benefits by Benefit Type

Aesthetic and other benefits—

Citywide, aesthetic/other benefits ranged from $1.1 to $1.6 billion, or $1,100 to $1,600 per tree over the 35-year period for the high- and low-mortality scenarios. This amount reflects the economic contribution of trees to property sales prices and retail sales, as well as other benefits such as beautification, privacy, wildlife habitat, sense of place, psychological and spiritual well-being.

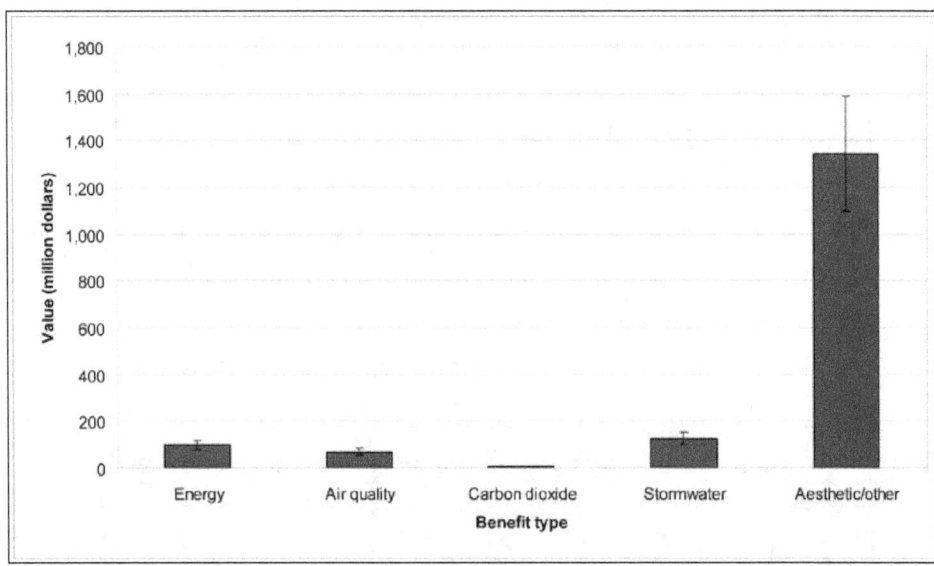

Figure 8—Total average value of benefits over the 35-year period by benefit type. Error bars show values for the low- and high-mortality scenarios.

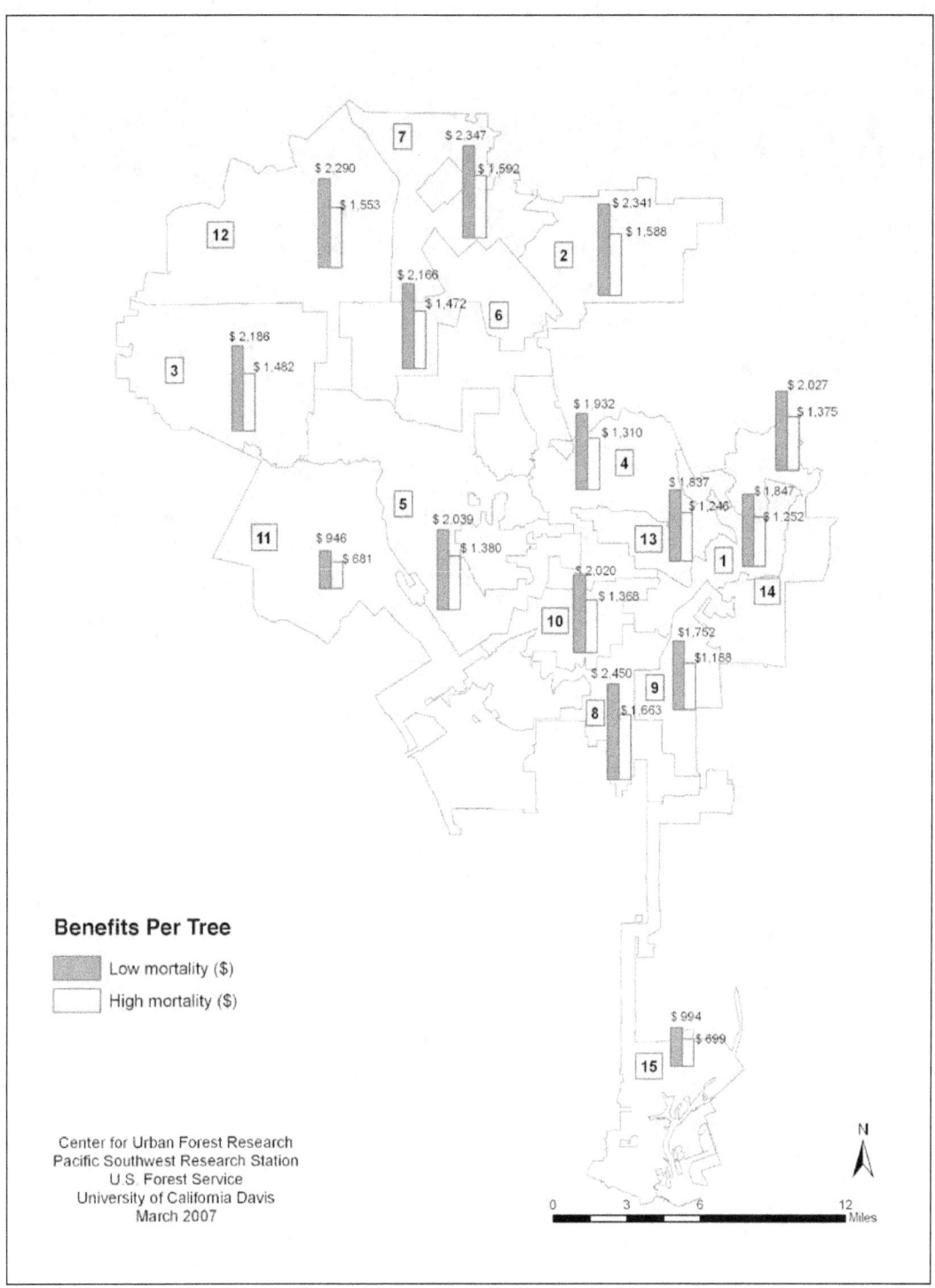

Figure 9— Average benefit per tree over the 35-year period for the low- and high-mortality scenarios.

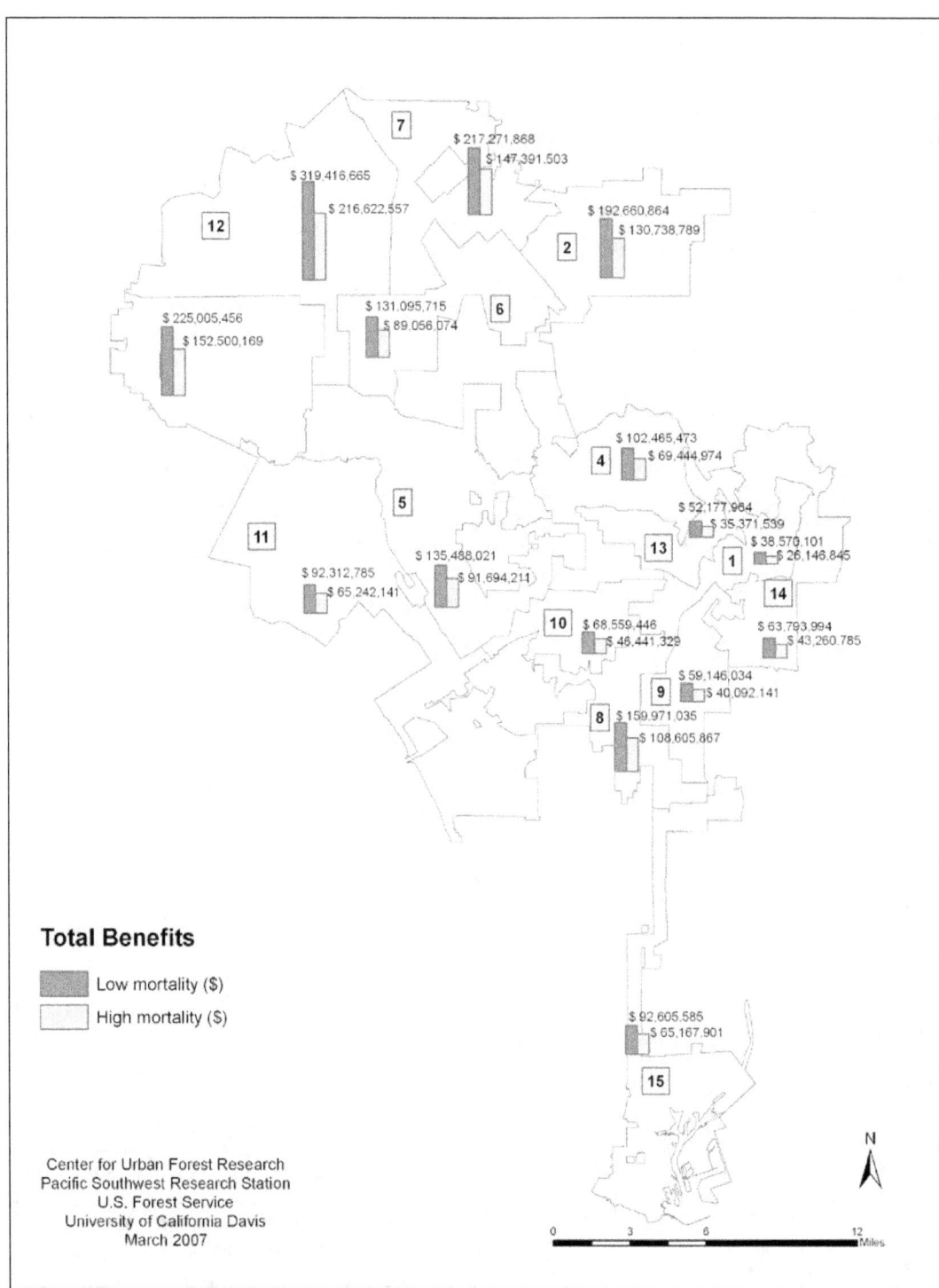

Figure 10— Total value of benefits over the 35-year period for the low- and high-mortality scenarios.

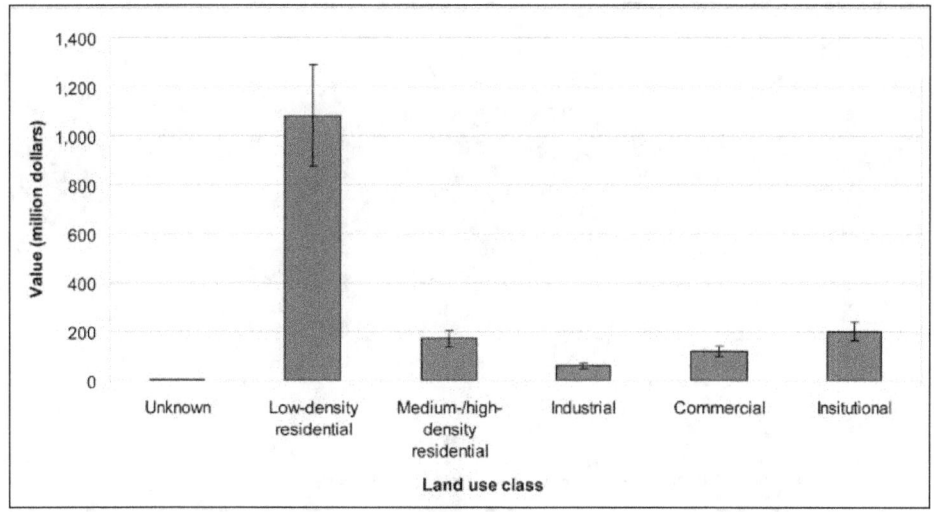

Figure 11—Total average value of benefits by land use class. Error bars show values for the low- and high-mortality scenarios.

Stormwater runoff reduction—

By intercepting rainfall in their crowns, trees reduce stormwater runoff and thereby protect water quality. Over the 35-year span of the project, 1 million trees will reduce runoff by approximately 17.4 billion gal (2.3 billion cubic feet; fig. 12). The value of this benefit is $125.3 million. The average annual interception rate per tree ranges from a low of 102 gal for the crapemyrtle (representative of small trees in the inland zone) to a high of 1,481 gal for the jacaranda (representative of medium trees in the inland zone). The difference is related to tree size and foliation period. The crapemyrtle is small at maturity and is deciduous during the rainy winter season, whereas the jacaranda develops a broad spreading crown and is in-leaf during the rainy season.

Energy-use reduction—

By shading residential buildings and lowering summertime air temperatures, the 1 million trees are projected to reduce electricity consumed for air conditioning by 917,000 MWh or $97 million (fig. 13). However, this cooling savings is partially offset by increased heating costs from tree shade that obstructs winter sunlight. Tree shade is expected to increase natural gas required for heating by 127,331 MBtu, which is valued at $851,000. Despite this cost, a net energy savings of $96 million is projected. The adverse effects of winter tree shade can be limited by strategically locating trees and selecting solar-friendly species for locations where solar access is a concern (McPherson et al. 2000, 2001).

Over its 35-year planning horizon, the 1-million-tree planting is projected to reduce atmospheric CO_2 by 1.02 million tons. Assuming this benefit is priced at $6.68 per ton, the corresponding value is $7.5 million.

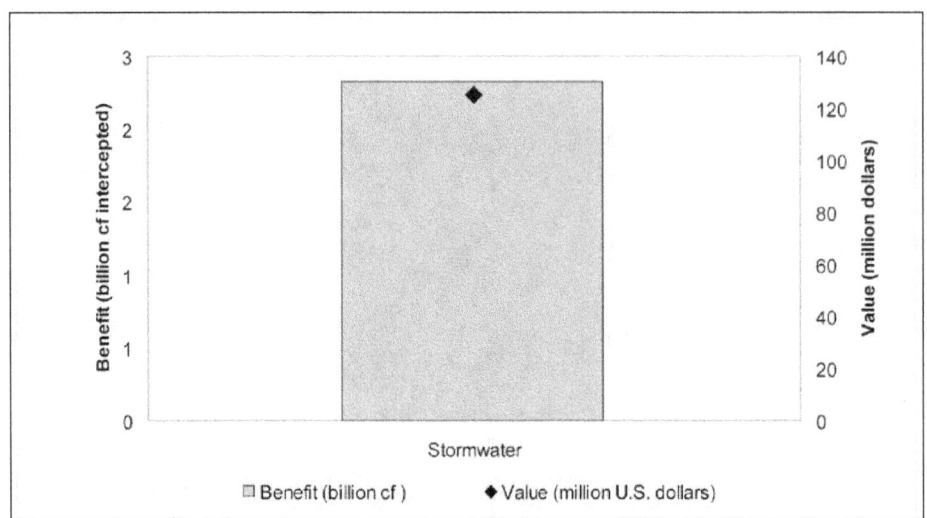

Figure 12—Total average value of stormwater runoff reduction benefits for the 35-year period.

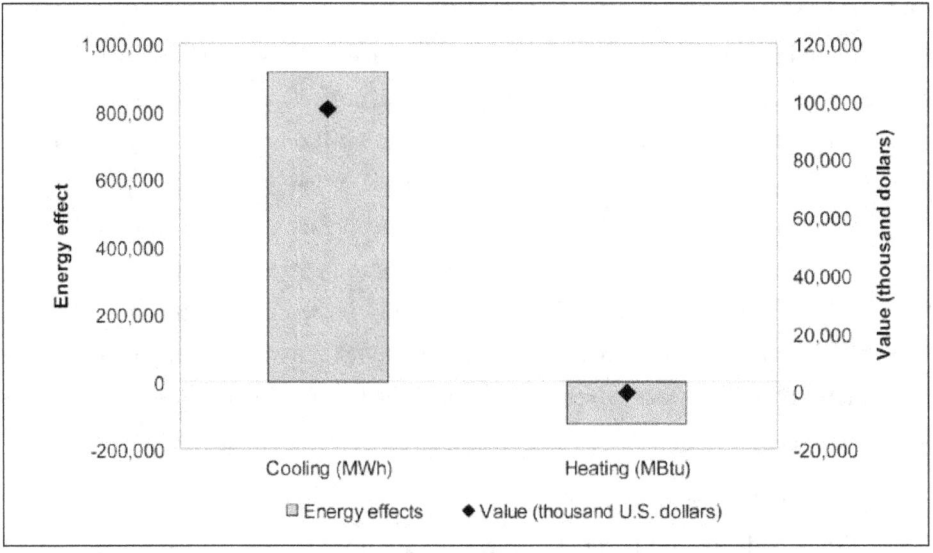

Figure 13—Total average value of tree effects on residential cooling (electricity, MWh) and heating (natural gas, MBtu) energy use for the 35-year period.

Atmospheric carbon dioxide reduction—

Over its 35-year planning horizon, the 1-million-tree planting is projected to reduce atmospheric CO_2 by 1.02 million tons (fig. 14). Assuming this benefit is priced at $6.68 per ton, the corresponding value is $7.5 million. Emission reductions at power plants associated with effects of the trees on building energy use (498,000 to 772,000 tons) are greater than biological sequestration of CO_2 by the trees themselves (389,000 to 598,000 tons). A relatively small amount of CO_2 is released during tree care and decomposition of dead biomass (101,000 to 123,000 tons). The CO_2 reduction benefit varies widely based on tree size. For example, in the inland zone for the low-mortality scenario, the small crapemyrtle annually sequesters and reduces emissions by only 5 and 55 lb per tree on average, compared to 220 and 150 lb for the large evergreen ash. Where space permits, strategically locating large trees to reduce home cooling costs will result in substantial benefits to mitigate climate change.

Air quality improvement—

By improving air quality, the tree planting will enhance human health and environmental quality in Los Angeles. This benefit is valued at $68 million over the 35-year planning horizon (fig. 15). Interception of PM_{10} and uptake of O_3 and NO_2 are especially valuable. The 1-million-tree planting project is estimated to intercept and reduce power plant emissions of PM_{10} by 2,365 tons over the 35-year period. The value of this benefit is $24 million, or 35 percent of total air quality benefits. For the low-mortality example, annual deposition rates average 0.14 to 0.19 lb per tree for the medium tree in coastal and inland zones, while corresponding emission reductions range from 0.04 to 0.12 lb.

The 1 million trees are projected to reduce O_3 by 3,121 tons, with average annual deposition rates ranging from 0.25 to 0.35 lb per medium tree in the low-mortality scenario for the coastal and inland zones, respectively. Ozone uptake is valued at $23 million over the project life, or 34 percent of total air quality benefits. Uptake of NO_2, an ozone precursor, is estimated at 2,494 tons, with a value of $18.7 million over the 35-year period. This benefit accounts for 27 percent of the total air quality benefit. A small amount of VOC emissions from power plants will be reduced because of energy savings. However, this analysis does not incorporate costs associated with biogenic VOCs, because all five species are low emitters.

Discussion

Comparison of Results

In Los Angeles, the existing TCC is 20.8 percent, which is close to the 20 percent TCC in Baltimore and 23 percent in New York City (table 14). This is surprising given Los Angeles's Mediterranean climate, which makes irrigation essential for establishment and growth of many tree species. However, the technical potential (existing TCC plus potential TCC) is much less in Los Angeles than reported for the other two cities. In Los Angeles, the technical potential (33 percent) represents only a 12-percent increase in TCC above the existing 21 percent. Hence, the PTCC is 57 percent of existing TCC. In New York City and Baltimore, the PTCC is 187

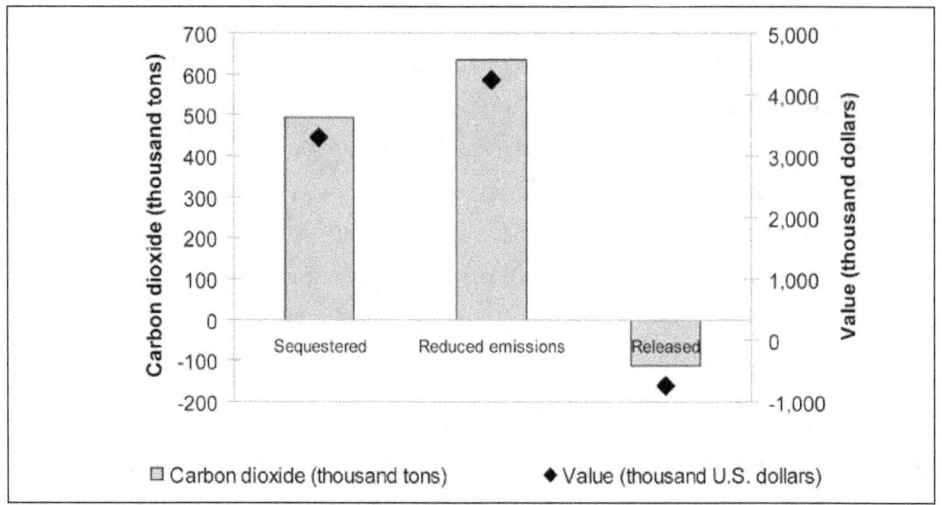

Figure 14—Total average value of carbon dioxide sequestration, emission reductions associated with energy effects, and release owing to tree care activities and decomposition of dead wood (1 short ton = 2,000 lb).

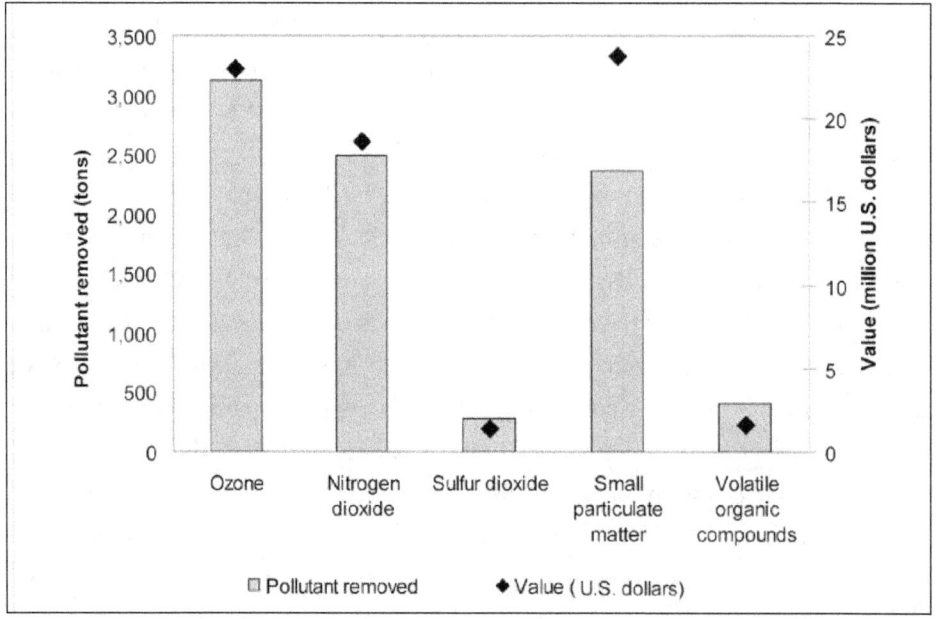

Figure 15—Total average value of tree effects on ozone, nitrogen dioxide, sulfur dioxide, particulate matter and volatile organic compounds. These values account for deposition to the tree canopy and emission reductions associated with energy effects.

Table 14—Tree canopy cover (percentage) results for three U.S. cities

City	Existing	Potential	Technical potential	Market potential
		Percent		
Los Angeles	21	12	33	28
New York City	23	43	66	30
Baltimore	20	53	73	40

percent and 265 percent times the existing TCC. This finding suggests that there is much less available growing space for trees in Los Angeles than in the other cities. Although we do not have a definitive explanation for this result, one reason may be the masking of mountain areas from our study site, which eliminated many potential tree planting sites.

In Los Angeles and Baltimore, the target TCC equals the existing TCC plus about one-half the difference between existing and technical PTCC. In New York City, the target is a much smaller percentage of the technical TCC. The lower target in New York City may reflect the fact that a larger proportion of PTCC is in open spaces where new plantings would conflict with existing uses such as ball fields and prairie landscapes.

We compared results of the benefits assessment with previous benefit-cost analyses in our tree guides for coastal southern California and Inland Empire communities (McPherson et al. 2000, 2001). We expected differences in results because the simulations for this study used more recent air quality data and median home sales prices, and different benefit prices and tree mortality rates. Nevertheless, the dollar values of average annual benefits compared well. In the coastal southern California tree guide, average annual benefits for the representative small and medium street trees were $22 and $48, compared to $38 for this study (low-mortality scenario). In the Inland Empire tree guide, the average annual benefit was $15 and $61 for the small and medium trees. In this study, the corresponding value was $56 (assumes 50 percent small, 41 percent medium, 9 percent large). Hence, benefit values reported here are reasonable when compared with previously reported findings from similar analyses for the same region.

Uncertainty and Limitations

There are several sources of error associated with these benefit projections. One source of error pertains to land cover classification. Inaccurate land cover classification results in inaccurate assessments of potential tree planting sites when pervious sites without trees are misclassified as having trees or as impervious, and impervious sites are misclassified as pervious and without trees. Our image classification assessment indicates that overall classification accuracy is 88.6 percent based on a pixel-by-pixel comparison.

Although ground-truthing of computer-based estimates of potential tree sites led to a calibration of the estimates, other errors can reduce the accuracy of estimates. For example, the computer-based method can miss potential tree sites in large open spaces because a limited number of iterations are run for each tree size class. Potential tree planting sites in parking lots in medium/high-density housing areas were not included. These types of limitations were observed during a workshop in Los Angeles when 15 sample areas were reviewed by local program participants. Computer-based tree sites were confirmed, deleted, and added based on local understanding of tree planting potential. Our informal findings were that the largest discrepancies between computer- and human-based potential tree sites were for institutional and industrial land uses, whereas estimates for residential land uses were in close agreement.

Modeling error influences the accuracy of benefit estimates. In this analysis we used three representative species in two climate zones, an obvious simplification of the actual tree planting program. In reality, over 100 species will be planted throughout the city, which has a myriad of microclimates. Therefore, these results are only accurate to the extent that the actual trees planted resemble the size and foliation characteristics of the species mix we have used here.

Our numerical models do not fully account for effects of BVOC emissions from trees on O_3 formation, or the effects of shade from new trees on VOC emissions from parked cars and other anthropogenic sources. We also have not simulated the effects of trees on nonresidential building energy use.

Over three-quarters of total value is for aesthetic and other benefits, and our understanding of this type of benefit is least certain. To estimate this value, we rely on research conducted in Georgia that may not be directly transferable to Los Angeles. Moreover, we assume that our value fully accounts for all the other benefits associated with city trees that have not been explicitly calculated.

The benefits quantified here should be considered a conservative estimate. They do not include many other benefits that are more difficult to translate into dollar terms.

The benefits quantified here should be considered a conservative estimate. They do not include many other benefits that are more difficult to translate into dollar terms. For example, tree shade on streets can help offset pavement management costs by protecting paving from weathering. The asphalt paving on streets contains stone aggregate in an oil binder. Tree shade lowers the street surface temperature and reduces heating and volatilization of the binder (McPherson and Muchnick 2005). As a result, the aggregate remains protected for a longer period by the oil binder. When unprotected, vehicles loosen the aggregate, and much like sandpaper, the loose aggregate grinds down the pavement. Because most weathering of asphalt-concrete pavement occurs during the first 5 to 10 years, when new street tree plantings provide little shade, this benefit mainly applies when older streets are resurfaced.

Scientific studies confirm our intuition that trees in cities provide social and psychological benefits. Views of trees and nature from homes and offices provide restorative experiences that ease mental fatigue and help people to concentrate (Kaplan and Kaplan 1989). Desk workers with a view of nature report lower rates of sickness and greater satisfaction with their jobs compared to those having no visual connection to nature (Kaplan 1992). Trees provide important settings for recreation and relaxation in and near cities. The act of planting trees can have social value, as bonds between people and local groups often result.

The presence of trees in cities provides public health benefits and improves the well-being of those who live, work, and play in cities. Physical and emotional stress has both short- and long-term effects. Prolonged stress can compromise the human immune system. A series of studies on human stress caused by general urban conditions and city driving show that views of nature reduce the stress response of both body and mind (Parsons et al. 1998). Urban green also appears to have an "immunization effect" in that people show less stress response if they have had a recent view of trees and vegetation. Hospitalized patients with views of nature and time spent outdoors need less medication, sleep better, have a better outlook, and recover more quickly than patients without connections to nature (Ulrich 1985). Skin cancer is a particular concern in sunny southern California. Trees reduce exposure to ultraviolet light, thereby lowering the risk of harmful effects from skin cancer and cataracts (Tretheway and Manthe 1999). Our accounting approach may not capture the full value of all benefits associated with a large-scale tree planting program in Los Angeles.

Dissemination of Data—

The GIS data on existing TCC and potential tree planting sites, as well as information on the projected benefits of 1 million new trees are valuable assets for the city and its residents. To manage and disseminate this information, we suggest the following:

- The city designate a central clearinghouse for GIS data related to the Million Trees LA program. Data from this and other studies could be accessed through the clearinghouse.

- Million Trees LA develop a handout that summarizes key points from this study, particularly the future benefits to be gained from investment in tree planting and stewardship.

- To document all aspects of this research and make it readily accessible, the Center for Urban Forest Research publish a General Technical Report, peer-reviewed and available at no cost to the public through the U.S. Forest Service.

- Important aspects of this study be summarized and posted on the Million Trees LA Web site.

Implementation of the program—

Information on the benefits of this large-scale tree planting program can be helpful in developing partnerships with investors. For example, corporations may invest in the program because they can report carbon credits from trees that help offset

To attract serious investment, the program will have to demonstrate that the benefits from these trees will be permanent and quantifiable. To do this will entail a commitment to accountability through annual monitoring and reporting.

their emissions. Similarly, if the South Coast Air Quality Management District includes trees as an air quality improvement measure in their State Implementation Plan, more funds for tree planting and management would become available. To capitalize on these opportunities, the Million Trees LA program will need a credible process for tracking tree planting and monitoring the survival, growth, and functionality of its trees. To attract serious investment, the program will have to demonstrate that the benefits from these trees will be permanent and quantifiable. To do this will entail a commitment to accountability through annual monitoring and reporting.

The Center for Urban Forest Research proposes working with Million Trees LA to develop a GIS Decision-Support System (GDSS) that provides a user-friendly interface for making use of the data from this study for planning and implementation of neighborhood tree planting projects by tree planting coordinators such as NorthEast Trees and TreePeople. The GDSS will allow users without extensive GIS experience to examine different parcels, select and locate trees to provide the greatest benefits, budget for planting and maintenance costs, project the future stream of benefits, assess the ecological stability of the planting at a population level, and track future tree survival and growth. The GDSS will help Los Angeles maximize its return on investment in tree planting through application of state-of-the-art science and technology. The project will require 1 year and cost approximately $175,000.

Approximately 20 percent of the target TCC for Los Angeles is paved parking lot area. Planting trees in parking lots poses technical and financial challenges. However, if done judiciously, there are opportunities for parking lot tree plantings to substantially improve air quality, reduce stormwater runoff, cool urban heat islands, and improve community attractiveness. To accomplish this, the program could establish new partnerships aimed at developing the technical specifications, financial means, and community support for a major parking lot greening effort in Los Angeles that could serve as a model for cities around the world.

The Center for Urban Forest Research proposes to collaborate with other scientists in southern California to study the effects of trees on the social, economic, and environmental health of Los Angeles and its nearly 4 million residents. In particular, we need to better understand:

- Barriers to tree planting and incentives for different markets
- Effects of trees on the urban heat island and air quality
- Effects of drought stress on tree survival and ability to remove air pollutants
- Primary causes of tree mortality

The Center for Urban Forest Research proposes to collaborate with other scientists in southern California to study the effects of trees on the social, economic, and environmental health of Los Angeles and its nearly 4 million residents.

- Best management practices to promote tree survival
- Citywide policy scenarios to promote urban tree canopy, neighborhood desirability, and economic development
- How to link TCC goals to other city goals: increasing community health, neighborhood quality of life, environmental literacy, and sustainability.

Future Research—

As the second largest city in the United States, Los Angeles manages an extensive municipal forest. Its management could set the standard for the region and the country. To do so, the Center for Urban Forest Research and the city of Los Angeles could cooperate to conduct a tree inventory and assessment that provides information on the existing urban forest:

- Structure (species composition, diversity, age distribution, condition, etc.)
- Function (magnitude of environmental and aesthetic benefits)
- Value (dollar value of benefits realized)
- Management needs (sustainability, maintenance, costs)
- Management recommendations aimed at increasing resource sustainability.

Los Angeles is a vibrant city that will continue to grow. As it grows it should also continue to invest in its tree canopy. This is no easy task given financial constraints and trends toward higher density development that may put space for trees at a premium. The challenge ahead is to better integrate the green infrastructure with the gray infrastructure by increasing tree planting, providing adequate space for trees, and designing plantings to maximize net benefits over the long term, thereby perpetuating a resource that is both functional and sustainable. The Center for Urban Forest Research looks forward to working with the city of Los Angeles and its many professionals to meet that challenge in the years ahead.

Common and Scientific Names

Common name	Scientific name
Camphor	*Cinnamomum camphora* (L.) J. Presl
Crapemyrtle	*Lagerstroemia indica* L.
Evergreen ash	*Fraxinus uhdei* (Wenzig) Lingelsh.
Jacaranda	*Jacaranda mimosifolia* D. Don
Yew	*Podocarpus macrophyllus* (Thunb.) Sweet

Acknowledgments

This research was supported by funds provided by the city of Los Angeles, California, and we thank Paula Daniels, George Gonzalez, and Lillian Kawasaki for their support. We wish to acknowledge Patrice Gin, Randy Price, and Kirk Bishop (Public Works / Bureau of Engineering / Mapping Division, city of Los Angeles) for sharing their GIS data and aerial imagery with us. Rebecca Drayse, Edith Ben-Horin, and David O'Donnell of TreePeople did an outstanding job ground-truthing field plots and organizing the December workshop. We could not have completed this study without their assistance. Dr. Stephanie Pincetl (U.S. Forest Service), Michael Galvin (Maryland Department of Natural Resources), and Paula Daniels provided helpful reviews of an earlier version of this report. Also, we appreciate the knowledge and time shared by over 30 participants in the 1-day workshop. Thanks to Dan Knapp, Los Angeles Conservation Corp, who assisted with development of the planting scenarios. Kelaine Vargas and Paula Peper at the U.S. Forest Service Center for Urban Forest Research provided technical and editorial assistance throughout the course of the study.

Metric Equivalents

When you know:	Multiply by:	To find:
Inches (in)	2.54	Centimeters (cm)
Feet (ft)	.305	Meters (m)
Square feet (ft^2)	.0929	Square meters (m^2)
Square miles (mi^2)	2.59	Square kilometers (km^2)
Cubic feet (ft^3)	.028	Cubic meters (m^3)
Acres	.404	Hectares (ha)
Gallons (gal)	.00378	Cubic meters (m^3)
Pounds (lb)	.454	Kilograms (kg)
Tons (ton)	.907	Metric tonne (t)
Thousand British thermal units (kBtu)	1.05	Megajoules (MJ)

References

Ambrosia, V.; Buechel, S.W.; Brass, J.A.; Peterson, J.R.; Davies, R.H.; Kane, R.J.; Spain, S. 1998. An integration of remote sensing, GIS, and information distribution for wildfire detection and management. Photogrammetric Engineering and Remote Sensing. 64(10): 977–985.

American Forests. 2002a. Projected benefits of community tree planting: a multi-site model urban forest project in Atlanta. Washington, DC. 12 p.

American Forests. 2002b. Urban ecological analysis for the Washington, DC, metropolitan area. Washington, DC. 16 p.

American Forests. 2002c. Urban ecological analysis, Roanoke, Virginia. Washington, DC. 8 p.

Anderson, L.M.; Cordell, H.K. 1988. Residential property values improve by landscaping with trees. Southern Journal of Applied Forestry. 9: 162–166.

Benjamin, M.T.; Winer, A.M. 1998. Estimating the ozone-forming potential of urban trees and shrubs. Atmospheric Environment. 32: 53–68.

Brenzel, K.N., ed. 2001. Sunset Western garden book. 7th ed. Menlo Park, CA: Sunset Books. 624 p.

California Association of Realtors. 2006. Median home sales prices in Los Angeles - December, 2006. http://www.car.org/index.php?id=MzcwNDg#. (March 5, 2007).

Condon, P.; Moriarty, S., eds. 1999. Second nature: adapting LAs landscape for sustainable living. Los Angeles: TreePeople. 116 p.

Galvin, M.F.; Grove, M.J.; O'Neil-Dunne, J. 2006. A report on Baltimore City's present and potential urban tree canopy. Annapolis, MD: Maryland Forest Service. 17 p.

Gauderman, W.J.; Avol, E.; Gilliland, F.; Vora, H.; Thomas, D.; Kiros, B.; McConnell, R.; Kuenzli, N.; Lurmann, F.; Rappaport, E.; Margolis, H.; Bates, D.; Peters, J. 2004. The effect of air pollution on lung development from 10 to 18 years of age. The New England Journal of Medicine. 351(11): 1057–1067.

Gauderman, W.J.; Avol, E.; Lurmann, F.; Kuenzli, N.; Gilliland, F.; Peters, J.; McConnell, R. 2005. Childhood asthma and exposure to traffic and nitrogen dioxide. Epidemiology. 16(6): 737–743.

Given, S.; Pendleton, L.H.; Boehm, A.B. 2006. Regional public health cost estimates of contaminated coastal waters: a case study of gastroenteritis at Southern California beaches. Environmental Science and Technology. 40: 4851–4858.

Goetz, S.J.; Wright, R.K.; Smith, A.J.; Zinecker, E.; Schaub, E. 2003. IKONOS imagery for resource management: tree cover, impervious surfaces, and riparian buffer analyses in the mid-Atlantic region. Remote Sensing of the Environment. 88: 195–208.

Gong, P.; Howarth, P.J. 1990. The use of structural information for improving land-cover classification accuracies at the rural-urban fringe. Photogrammetric Engineering and Remote Sensing. 56(1): 67–73.

Gonzalez, S. 2004. Personal communication. Assistant maintenance superintendent, City of Vallejo, 111 Amador St., Vallejo, CA 94590.

Grove, J.M.; O'Neil-Dunne, J.; Pelletier, K.; Nowak, D.; Walton, J. 2006. A report on New York City's present and possible urban tree canopy. South Burlington, VT: U.S. Department of Agriculture, Forest Service, Northeastern Research Station. 25 p.

Irani, F.W.; Galvin, M.F. 2003. Strategic urban forests assessment: Baltimore, Maryland. In: Technology: converging at the top of the world. Proceedings of the American Society of Photogrammetry and Remote Sensing annual conference, Bethesda, MD: American Society of Photogrammetry and Remote Sensing: 85–94.

Jones & Stokes Associates, Inc. 1998. Cost-benefit analysis for the T.R.E.E.S. project. Sacramento, CA. 152 p.

Kaler, D.; Ray, C. 2005. City of Vancouver canopy report, GIS analysis using 2002 LIDAR. Vancouver, WA: Clark County GIS Division and Vancouver-Clark Parks and Recreation. 32 p.

Kaplan, R. 1992. Urban forestry and the workplace. In: Gobster, P.H., ed. Managing urban and high-use recreation settings. Gen. Tech. Rep. NC-163. St. Paul, MN: U.S. Department of Agriculture, Forest Service, North Central Research Station: 41–45.

Kaplan, R.; Kaplan, S. 1989. The experience of nature: a psychological perspective. Cambridge, United Kingdom: Cambridge University Press. 352 p.

Kellert, S.R.; Wilson, W.O., eds. 1993. The biophilia hypothesis. New York: Island Press. 483 p.

Kohavi, R.; Provost, F. 1998. Glossary of terms. Machine Learning. 30: 271–274.

Kollin, C. 2006. How green infrastructure measures up to structural stormwater services. Stormwater. 7(5): 138–144.

Lakshmi, V.; Murthy, M.; Dutt, C. 1998. Efficient forest resources management through GIS and remote sensing. Current Science. 75(3): 272–282.

Luley, C.J.; Bond, J. 2002. A plan to integrate management of urban trees into air quality planning. Report to the North East State Foresters Association. Naples, NY: Davey Resource Group. 61 p.

McBride, J.R.; Jacobs, D.F. 1986. Presettlement forest structure as a factor in urban forest development. Urban Ecology. 9(3–4): 245–266.

McPherson, E.G. 1992. Accounting for benefits and costs of urban greenspace. Landscape and Urban Planning. 22: 41–51.

McPherson, E.G. 1993. Evaluating the cost effectiveness of shade trees for demand-side management. The Electricity Journal. 6(9): 57–65.

McPherson, E.G. 1998. Structure and sustainability of Sacramento's urban forest. Journal of Forestry. 24(4): 174–190.

McPherson, E.G. 2001. Sacramento's parking lot shading ordinance: environmental and economic costs of compliance. Landscape and Urban Planning. 57: 105–123.

McPherson, E.G.; Muchnick, J. 2005. Effects of tree shade on asphalt concrete pavement performance. Journal of Arboriculture. 31(6): 303–309.

McPherson, E.G.; Simpson, J.R. 1999. Guidelines for calculating carbon dioxide reductions through urban forestry programs. Gen. Tech. Rep. PSW-171. Albany, CA: U.S. Department of Agriculture, Forest Service, Pacific Southwest Research Station. 237 p.

McPherson, E.G.; Simpson, J.R.; Peper, P.J.; Scott, K.I.; Xiao, Q. 2000. Tree guidelines for coastal southern California communities. Sacramento, CA: Local Government Commission. 98 p.

McPherson, E.G.; Simpson, J.R.; Peper, P.J.; Xiao, Q.; Pittenger, D.R.; Hodel, D.R. 2001. Tree guidelines for Inland Empire communities. Sacramento, CA: Local Government Commission. 116 p.

Montgomery County. 2000. Forest preservation strategy, a task force report. Rockville, MD: County of Montgomery. 16 p.

Myeong, S.; Nowak, D.J.; Hopkins, P.F.; Brock, R.H. 2001. Urban cover mapping using digital, high-spatial resolution aerial imagery. Urban Ecosystems. 5: 243–256.

Nowak, D.J.; Rowntree, R.A.; McPherson, E.G.; Sisinni, S.M.; Kerkmann, E.R.; Stevens, J.C. 1996. Measuring and analyzing urban tree cover. Landscape and Urban Planning. 36: 49–57.

Nowak, D.J.; Crane, D.E.; Stevens, J.C.; Hoehn, R. 2003. The Urban Forest Effects (UFORE) model: field data collection procedures. Syracuse, NY: U.S. Department of Agriculture, Forest Service. 30 p.

Parsons, R.; Tassinary, L.G.; Ulrich, R.S.; Hebl, M.R.; Grossman-Alexander, M. 1998. The view from the road: implications for stress recovery and immunization. Journal of Environmental Psychology. 18(2): 113–140.

Pearce, D. 2003. The social cost of carbon and its policy implications. Oxford Review of Economic Policy. 19(3): 362–384.

Pillsbury, N.H.; Reimer, J.L.; Thompson, R.P. 1998. Tree volume equations for fifteen urban species in California. Tech. Rep. 7. San Luis Obispo, CA: Urban Forest Ecosystems Institute, California Polytechnic State University. 56 p.

Poracsky, J.; Lackner, M. 2004. Urban forest canopy cover in Portland, Oregon, 1972–2002: final report. Portland, OR: Geography Department, Portland State University. 38 p.

Price, K.; Guo, X.; Stiles, J. 2002. Optimal Landsat TM band combinations and vegetation indices for discrimination of six grassland types in eastern Kansas. International Journal of Remote Sensing. 23(23): 5031–5042.

Sanders, R.A. 1984. Some determinants of urban forest structure. Urban Ecology. 8: 13–27.

Sarkovich, M. 2006. Personal communication. Demand-side specialist, Sacramento Municipal Utility District, 1708 59th St., Sacramento, CA 95817-1889.

Scott, K.I.; McPherson, E.G.; Simpson, J.R. 1998. Air pollutant uptake by Sacramento's urban forest. Journal of Arboriculture. 24(4): 224–234.

Shao, G.; Young, D.; Porter, J.; Hayden, B. 1998. An integration of remote sensing and GIS to examine the responses of shrub thicket distributions to shoreline changes on Virginia Barrier Islands. Journal of Coastal Research. 14(1): 299–307.

Tou, J.T.; Gonzalez, R.C. 1974. Pattern recognition principles. Reading, MA: Addison-Wesley.

Tretheway, R.; Manthe, A. 1999. Skin cancer prevention: another good reason to plant trees. In: McPherson, E.G.; Mathis, S., eds. Proceedings of the Best of the West summit. Davis, CA: University of California: 72–75.

Ulrich, R.S. 1985. Human responses to vegetation and landscapes. Landscape and Urban Planning. 13: 29–44.

Urban Forestry Task Force. 2003. Urban forestry plan, an element of the vision plan. Roanoke, VA: City of Roanoke. 41 p.

U.S. Department of Commerce, Census Bureau [U.S. Census Bureau]. 2000. Population finder, Census 2000. http://www.census.gov/. (27 March 2007).

Wang, M.Q.; Santini, D.J. 1995. Monetary values of air pollutant emissions in various U.S. regions. Transportation Research Record 1475: 33–41.

Xiao, Q.; McPherson, E.G.; Simpson, J.R.; Ustin, S.L. 2000. Winter rainfall interception by two mature open grown trees in Davis, California. Hydrological Processes. 14(4): 763–784.

Xiao, Q.; McPherson, E.G. 2005. Tree health mapping with multispectral remote sensing data at UC Davis, California. Urban Ecosystems 8: 349–361.

Xiao, Q.; Ustin, S.L.; McPherson, E.G. 2004. Using AVIRIS data and multiple-masking techniques to map urban forest species. International Journal of Remote Sensing. 25(24): 5637–5654.

Appendix

Table 15—Land cover distributions by neighborhood council[a]

Neighborhood councils	Area	Tree canopy cover		Irrigated grass cover		Dry grass/bare soil		Impervious/other		Mountain
	Acres	Acres	Percent	Acres	Percent	Acres	Percent	Acres	Percent	Acres
Arleta	2,089	350	16.8	217	10.4	231	11.1	1,291	61.8	
Arroyo Seco	1,698	781	46.0	64	3.8	145	8.5	708	41.7	523
Atwater Village	1,305	188	14.4	180	13.8	62	4.7	874	66.9	
Bel Air-Beverly Crest	6,964	3,715	53.3	699	10.0	194	2.8	2,356	33.8	3,997
Boyle Heights	3,668	418	11.4	278	7.6	46	1.3	2,926	79.8	
Canoga Park	2,361	357	15.1	208	8.8	135	5.7	1,660	70.3	
Central Alameda	861	84	9.8	86	10.0	34	4.0	616	71.5	
Central Hollywood	786	66	8.3	21	2.7	11	1.4	689	87.6	0
Central San Pedro	1,386	134	9.7	91	6.6	67	4.8	1,094	79.0	0
Chatsworth	5,348	909	17.0	659	12.3	454	8.5	3,327	62.2	1,950
Coastal San Pedro	2,287	233	10.2	515	22.5	174	7.6	1,365	59.7	2
Community and Neighbors for Ninth District Unity	1,632	126	7.7	196	12.0	34	2.1	1,276	78.2	
Del Rey	1,942	192	9.9	259	13.3	34	1.7	1,457	75.0	0
Downtown Los Angeles	3,214	95	3.0	74	2.3	27	0.8	3,017	93.9	2
Eagle Rock	2,323	801	34.5	105	4.5	179	7.7	1,238	53.3	321
Elysian Valley Riverside	459	47	10.2	30	6.5	28	6.2	338	73.7	
Empowerment Congress Central Area ndc	1,812	192	10.6	371	20.5	98	5.4	1,152	63.6	
Empowerment Congress North Area	2,455	289	11.8	281	11.5	104	4.2	1,781	72.5	
Empowerment Congress Southeast Area	2,725	270	9.9	481	17.7	42	1.6	1,915	70.3	
Empowerment Congress Southwest Area	1,708	135	7.9	401	23.5	44	2.6	1,127	66.0	1
Empowerment Congress West area	2,091	279	13.3	458	21.9	78	3.7	1,276	61.0	0
Encino	7,361	2,293	31.2	1,253	17.0	247	3.4	3,583	48.7	1,337
Foothill Trails District	4,010	958	23.9	341	8.5	624	15.6	2,086	52.0	8,368
Glassell Park	1,531	292	19.0	209	13.7	120	7.8	910	59.5	97
Granada Hills North	4,600	1,191	25.9	644	14.0	454	9.9	2,311	50.2	2,770
Grass Roots Venice	2,048	334	16.3	177	8.6	7	0.4	1,529	74.7	1
Greater Cypress Park	787	122	15.5	38	4.8	64	8.1	563	71.5	41
Greater Echo Park Elysian	2,324	390	16.8	413	17.8	123	5.3	1,370	59.0	370
Greater Griffith Park	3,528	964	27.3	664	18.8	232	6.6	1,561	44.3	2,356
Greater Toluca Lake	961	308	32.0	152	15.8	26	2.7	476	49.5	
Greater Wilshire	2,538	682	26.9	379	14.9	108	4.2	1,370	54.0	
Harbor City	1,565	245	15.7	260	16.6	88	5.6	971	62.0	0
Harbor Gateway North	2,029	244	12.0	370	18.2	33	1.6	1,378	67.9	0
Harbor Gateway South	2,062	177	8.6	316	15.3	34	1.6	1,535	74.4	0
Historic Cultural	1,369	81	5.9	59	4.3	38	2.8	1,148	83.8	166

(Continues on next page)

Land cover distributions by neighborhood council[a] *(Continued)*

Neighborhood councils	Area	Tree canopy cover		Irrigated grass cover		Dry grass/bare soil		Impervious/other		Mountain
	Acres	*Acres*	*Percent*	*Acres*	*Percent*	*Acres*	*Percent*	*Acres*	*Percent*	*Acres*
Historic Highland Park	2,423	648	26.7	48	2.0	140	5.8	1,313	54.2	274
Hollywood Hills West	3,525	1,278	36.3	363	10.3	145	4.1	1,635	46.4	1,330
Hollywood United	1,468	532	36.3	93	6.3	61	4.2	694	47.3	752
LA-32	2,665	732	27.5	82	3.1	229	8.6	1,577	59.2	443
Lincoln Heights	1,893	253	13.4	47	2.5	67	3.6	1,491	78.8	93
Macarthur	334	20	6.0	24	7.2	8	2.4	282	84.5	
Mar Vista	2,671	611	22.9	291	10.9	52	1.9	1,638	61.3	0
Mid City	1,113	137	12.3	102	9.2	61	5.5	813	73.0	
Mid City West	2,641	457	17.3	253	9.6	95	3.6	1,835	69.5	1
Mid-town North Hollywood	3,030	545	18.0	265	8.7	121	4.0	2,100	69.3	
Mission Hills	2,302	422	18.3	286	12.4	361	15.7	1,233	53.6	
Nc Valley Village	1,257	346	27.6	142	11.3	51	4.1	717	57.1	
North Hills West	2,212	507	22.9	432	19.5	130	5.9	1,208	54.6	
North Hollywood North East	1,930	232	12.0	141	7.3	91	4.7	1,466	76.0	
Northridge East	2,566	519	20.2	479	18.7	176	6.9	1,419	55.3	
Northridge West	2,556	435	17.0	469	18.4	215	8.4	1,433	56.1	35
Northwest San Pedro	2,431	277	11.4	528	21.7	198	8.1	1,362	56.0	0
Old Northridge	857	122	14.3	103	12.0	57	6.7	574	67.0	
Olympic Park	724	97	13.4	75	10.3	41	5.7	512	70.6	
P.I.C.O.	1,155	165	14.3	132	11.4	73	6.4	785	67.9	
Pacoima	3,852	474	12.3	239	6.2	477	12.4	2,612	67.8	931
Palms	571	45	7.8	34	5.9	14	2.4	479	83.9	
Park Mesa Heights	1,818	170	9.3	396	21.8	84	4.6	1,168	64.2	1
Pico Union	1,026	103	10.0	68	6.6	24	2.3	831	81.0	
Porter Ranch	2,394	276	11.5	586	24.5	216	9.0	1,316	55.0	1,294
Reseda	3,759	649	17.3	556	14.8	294	7.8	2,259	60.1	
Sherman Oaks	5,016	1,720	34.3	552	11.0	176	3.5	2,567	51.2	527
Silver Lake	1,839	409	22.2	242	13.1	67	3.7	901	49.0	
South Robertson	1,682	332	19.7	191	11.4	74	4.4	1,086	64.5	0
Southeast/Central Ave	1,662	107	6.5	98	5.9	43	2.6	1,414	85.1	0
Studio City	3,403	1,420	41.7	303	8.9	82	2.4	1,580	46.4	528
Sun Valley Area	5,260	551	10.5	251	4.8	245	4.7	4,208	80.0	314
Sunland-Tujunga	3,613	1,093	30.3	344	9.5	320	8.9	1,856	51.4	4,024
Sylmar	6,957	1,185	17.0	760	10.9	1,212	17.4	3,799	54.6	963
Tarzana	4,282	1,290	30.1	776	18.1	285	6.7	1,932	45.1	779
United neighborhoods of the Historic Arlington Heights, West Adams, and Jefferson Park Community	1,772	205	11.6	138	7.8	84	4.7	1,345	75.9	
Valley Glen CC	2,443	608	24.9	301	12.3	129	5.3	1,405	57.5	
Van Nuys	3,757	695	18.5	328	8.7	154	4.1	2,580	68.7	
Vermont Harbor	1,396	151	10.8	176	12.6	60	4.3	1,009	72.3	
Vernon/Main	1,346	123	9.1	134	9.9	55	4.1	1,035	76.9	
Watts	1,294	168	13.0	226	17.4	77	5.9	824	63.7	0

(Continues on next page)

Land cover distributions by neighborhood council[a] *(Continued)*

Neighborhood councils	Area	Tree canopy cover		Irrigated grass cover		Dry grass/bare soil		Impervious/other		Mountain
	Acres	*Acres*	*Percent*	*Acres*	*Percent*	*Acres*	*Percent*	*Acres*	*Percent*	*Acres*
West Adams	1,387	168	12.1	152	10.9	75	5.4	992	71.5	0
West Hills	4,569	1,238	27.1	657	14.4	114	2.5	2,561	56.0	1,402
West LA	1,197	133	11.1	68	5.7	33	2.7	964	80.5	0
West Van Nuys/Lake Balboa	5,640	614	10.9	546	9.7	118	2.1	2,416	42.8	
Westchester/Playa del Ray	9,170	1,170	12.8	1,887	20.6	333	3.6	5,721	62.4	1
Westside	2,405	606	25.2	361	15.0	110	4.6	1,328	55.2	2
Wilmington	6,033	303	5.0	208	3.4	219	3.6	4,496	74.5	673
Wilshire Center - Koreatown	1,485	111	7.5	48	3.3	35	2.3	1,284	86.5	
Winnetka	2,827	538	19.0	387	13.7	234	8.3	1,668	59.0	
Woodland Hills-Warner Center	9,122	2,785	30.5	1,175	12.9	561	6.1	4,600	50.4	806

[a] Some neighborhood council boundaries overlap.